Fire and Wind is for people who keep the Holy Spirit at arm's length because they have been taught that you shouldn't talk about the Holy Spirit. It's also for those who sometimes talk too much about the Holy Spirit. Most of all, *Fire & Wind* is written for people who long for the power and presence of the Holy Spirit in their lives.

—**Mark Batterson**, *New York Times* bestselling author of *The Circle Maker*; lead pastor of National Community Church

Start to finish, I nodded in agreement with so much of what Stan Jantz wrote in *Fire and Wind*. We have classics that theologians have written on the Holy Spirit, which Stan references. We have books by pastors on the Holy Spirit, which Stan quotes. But in *Fire and Wind*, we get a refreshing and personally touching perspective on the Holy Spirit by a Bible-loving Jesus follower whose heart has been stirred in recent years over what he has missed much of his life. In this easy-to-read book, Stan unpacks theological truths of the Spirit while he also encourages us to experience in new ways the power of the Spirit.

—**Barry H. Corey**, president of Biola University and author of *Love Kindness*

The phrase "Holy Spirit" can't help but evoke an emotional reaction for us, ranging from happiness to awe to confusion. With so many theories about how the Spirit works and moves in us, it can be a bit overwhelming. Stan Jantz's book clarifies in a fresh way what the Bible, great experts from the past, and his own experience say about how we can connect on a deep and authentic level to the most misunderstood Person of the Trinity. Highly recommended.

—**John Townsend**, Ph.D., *New York Times* bestselling author of the Boundaries book series; founder, Townsend Institute for Leadership and Counseling

Stan Jantz is one of my favorite authors. He is biblical, insightful, and enjoyable to read. In *Fire and Wind*, he takes a fresh approach to the question of how the Holy Spirit is present and active in our lives. I hope you will read it with an open mind and consider that God may be active in ways you have never imagined.

—**Sean McDowell**, Biola University professor, popular speaker, and coauthor of *So the Next Generation Will Know*

FIRE

&

WIND

STAN JANTZ

HARVEST HOUSE PUBLISHERS
EUGENE, OREGON

Published in association with The Steve Laube Agency, LLC, 24 W. Camelback Road A-635, Phoenix, Arizona 85013.

Cover photo © Bernardo Ramonfaur / shutterstock

Cover design by Studio Gearbox

Fire and Wind
Copyright © 2020 by Stan Jantz
Published by Harvest House Publishers
Eugene, Oregon 97408
www.harvesthousepublishers.com

ISBN 978-0-7369-7777-7 (pbk.)
ISBN 978-0-7369-7778-4 (eBook)

Library of Congress Cataloging-in-Publication Data

Names: Jantz, Stan, author.
Title: Fire and wind / Stan Jantz.
Description: Eugene : Harvest House Publishers, 2019.
Identifiers: LCCN 2019017567 (print) | ISBN 9780736977777 (pbk.)
Subjects: LCSH: Holy Spirit.
Classification: LCC BT121.3 .J345 2019 (print) | LCC BT121.3 (ebook) | DDC 231/.3--dc23
LC record available at https://lccn.loc.gov/2019017567
LC ebook record available at https://lccn.loc.gov/2019980325

Printed in the United States of America

19 20 21 22 23 24 25 26 27 / VP-SK / 10 9 8 7 6 5 4 3 2 1

Contents

Introduction

My name is Stan, and I have ignored the Holy Spirit for too long.

It's not like I've *purposely* ignored or shunned him. Throughout my life, I have simply forgotten about the Holy Spirit; I just haven't thought about him all that much on a personal level. God the Father has been my focus, along with Jesus and the Bible. I guess you could say I'm one of those Christians who live as if the three members of the Trinity are the Father, Son, and Holy Bible.

Here's how it worked for me. I believed in God at an early age and accepted Jesus as my Savior by the time I was seven years old. As I grew up, nurtured by godly parents and a series of pastors who were skilled at teaching the Bible, I matured in my faith. I did my best to read and study the Bible while following the command, "Love the Lord your God with all your heart and with all your soul and with all your mind and with all your strength" (Mark 12:30 NIV).

Eventually Jesus became my one true spiritual passion, and how can he not be? Being saved is all about Jesus. As for the

Holy Spirit, I knew he was there, but I didn't know what to do with him. So he just sat quietly in my heart and soul (while I directed my mind and strength to God and Jesus), waiting patiently for me to give him a little nod—you know, one of those glances where you look at someone and give them that slight upward thrust of your chin—just to let him know that I knew he was there. Sadly, I didn't do all that much nodding in the Holy Spirit's direction.

So why did I write this book about the Holy Spirit? If the subject of the book has been sitting in the corner of my spiritual life, without me giving him so much as a glance, why do this now? Because I discovered something that changed my life. Actually, two somethings. One was definitely the Holy Spirit, but there was something else that prompted me to change the way I looked at this whole matter.

Not long ago I was at the point where my spiritual life was stagnant and predictable. I thought about the reason Jesus came to earth—"I came that they may have life and have it abundantly" (John 10:10 ESV)—and I concluded that my life wasn't all that abundant. Oh, I was doing fine in other areas, but spiritually I was feeling flat. Uninspired. And I figured that maybe the Holy Spirit was the key to this life I was missing. I can't tell you why he entered my mind, but something changed, like a light being turned on in a dark room.

So I said to the Holy Spirit, "It's time I got to know you better. I know *about* you, but I don't really *know* you." And the Holy Spirit said, "I'm ready if you are. Let's do something together."

Okay, so I didn't actually hear audible words, but I heard *his voice* speaking to me in my soul, telling me I've been missing something deeply meaningful, something that would change my life dramatically the moment I was willing and ready to experience the Holy Spirit as more than a doctrinal reality or principle or thought. If I was willing to hear him, the Holy Spirit was ready to speak. I didn't come to this conclusion on my own. The devotional writer A.W. Tozer helped me with this comment: "Of all the voices God uses to speak to us, the Spirit is the clearest and loudest."[1] I wanted to hear God's voice loud and clear, so that was the first reason I turned my mind—and eventually my heart, soul, and strength—to the Holy Spirit.

THE BOX IN THE ATTIC

There was a second factor that changed the way I looked at the Holy Spirit, and it wasn't all that spiritual. In fact, it was quite material. It was a cardboard box. Not just any box, but one filled with books that belonged to my father. My mother kept the box after my father died. I didn't know about it until my mother passed away and I collected her belongings, including this nondescript box containing about a dozen of my father's favorite books.

Even then, when it came into my possession, I put the box in the attic with the idea that I would look through it "someday." That day came a year ago when I stumbled across the box on a Saturday morning while doing some spring cleaning. I decided to look inside.

Besides being old, the books were alike in that they carried a single theme. They were all about the Holy Spirit. And because the books were old, they were written by authors who aren't exactly at the top of today's best-seller lists—Andrew Murray, D.L. Moody, A.B. Simpson, R.A. Torrey, A.W. Tozer.

As I pulled the books out of the box one by one, their titles immediately told me what they were about: *Experiencing the Holy Spirit*; *Secret Power*; *The Holy Spirit: Power from on High*; *The Person and Work of the Holy Spirit*; and *The Pursuit of God*.

As I thumbed through these volumes, I discovered that my father had underlined them extensively. In red ink. Several passages grabbed my attention. Even more, they stirred my heart.

> For a healthy Christian life, it is indispensable that we be fully conscious that we have received the Holy Spirit to dwell in us (Andrew Murray).[2]

> I believe that, although Christian men and women have the Holy Spirit dwelling in them, He is not dwelling within them in power. In other words, God has a great many sons and daughters without power (D.L. Moody).[3]

> Some of us are shivering and wondering why the Holy Spirit does not fill us. We have plenty coming in, but we do not give it out. Give out the blessing you have; start larger plans for service and blessing. You will soon find that the Holy Ghost is before you, and that He will present you with blessings for goodness and will give you all that He can trust you to give away to others (A.B. Simpson).[4]

> If we think of the Holy Spirit, as so many do, as merely a power or influence, our constant thought will be, *How can I get more of the Holy Spirit*, but if we think of Him in the biblical way as a divine

person, our thought will rather be, *How can the Holy Spirit have more of me?* (R.A. Torrey).[5]

There must be surrender to the Spirit of God, for His work is to show us the Father and the Son. If we cooperate with Him in loving obedience, God will manifest Himself to us, and that manifestation will be the difference between a nominal Christian life and a life radiant with the light of His face (A.W. Tozer).[6]

As I read such words, a desire suddenly stirred within my being. You could say my spirit was quickened. Instantly I had a desire not just to know about the Holy Spirit, but to know him like my father did. Like Murray, Moody, Simpson, Torrey, and Tozer knew the Holy Spirit.

SOMETHING STRANGE

There was something strange about my encounter with the Holy Spirit and my father's box of books. I had never been a Holy Spirit person. No one ever said, "Stan is charismatic." And until I opened that cardboard box, I didn't know my father had such an overriding interest in the Holy Spirit. It wasn't as much confusing as it was so different from anything I had previously experienced in my Christian life.

I suppose if the box had contained books by so-called "health and wealth" (prosperity) preachers, I would have dismissed them and wondered where my father had gone off the rails. But these were books by people who didn't fit the stereotype of today's typical charismatic writers. They lived and wrote in the latter part of the nineteenth century and the early twentieth century. They were and are respected writers on the Christian life. Murray, Moody, Simpson, Torrey, and Tozer were missionaries, evangelists, pastors, educators, and—of course—writers. And they all wrote deeply and profoundly on the importance of the Holy Spirit in the life of the believer. (A minibiography of each of these five writers is included at the end of this book.)

Over the next several months I read all the books in my father's box, plus many more about the Holy Spirit that were new to me. I searched the Scriptures for verses about the Holy Spirit. Most were familiar, but because I was reading them in a new light, they took on fresh meaning. In addition to reading, I prayed—only now I included the Holy Spirit in my prayers. I knew he could speak to me through the Word of God, but now he also spoke to me through prayer. I could hear his voice.

Before you conclude that I am some superspiritual person oozing with Holy Spirit goodness, eager to tell you all I know, it's time to reveal my true self: I am nobody special. Sometimes when I think about my failings and inadequacies, I feel like stopping this project and continuing on my spiritual journey in private. But that's not what the Spirit of God is asking me to do.

I believe the things I am learning and experiencing are not for me only, but for others like me who grew up in a church tradition that kept the Holy Spirit under wraps, in a corner, or completely outside the building.

I hope this book is also useful for those in the Pentecostal and charismatic tradition who already embrace the Holy Spirit, but perhaps are looking for a more meaningful experience with him.

And if I may be so bold, I pray that those who have rarely,

if ever, gone to church but are curious about this supernatural side of the Christian life that seems a little strange, but at the same time uniquely compelling, may find this book intriguing.

Truthfully, I'm probably only a little farther along on this new journey than you are. I'm not a wise teacher of the Holy Spirit. At best, I am a witness to the Holy Spirit's power and presence—his fire and wind. And I am willing and eager to continue to grow in this dimension of the Christian life that is so often overlooked and sometimes overemphasized. I hope that's enough for you to know in order to continue reading.

Ideally you and I would have a conversation over coffee so we could share impressions and thoughts about the Holy Spirit. We can't do that, but we can still have a connection. If you have put your faith in God, believing by faith that Jesus saved you, the Holy Spirit is in your life just as surely as he is in mine. That means we have a special spiritual bond that transcends physical space and time.

If you aren't yet a Christian, we still have something in common. As you will discover, even though the Holy Spirit may not be in you, he is not far from you. I believe with all my heart that you have picked up this book because the Holy Spirit is drawing you to something wonderful and supernatural and life-changing through your inner being: your thoughts, your will, and your heart.

As you read this book, I encourage you to set a goal for yourself. As I once did, you might be tempted to set this kind of goal: "to get more of the Holy Spirit in my life." But I recommend you set a more appropriate goal, like this one suggested by R.A. Torrey: "to give more of myself to the Holy Spirit."

HOW TO USE THIS BOOK

If your goal is to give more of yourself to the Holy Spirit, it will be important to know how he interacts with you every day, every hour, every moment. I will share what I have learned from Scripture, from others (including the authors of those books in my father's box), and from my experience. We'll start at the beginning, when as a Christian you first encounter the Holy Spirit, and then we'll progress on a spiritual journey through several chapters—or stages of your life—with the Holy Spirit.

In chapter 1 we will address who the Holy Spirit is, including his relationship to God the Father and Jesus the Son. Consider this a kind of orientation so you have a basic understanding of the Holy Spirit's role in the eternal, spiritual world and why he matters in your life here on earth. We will address some misconceptions people have about the Holy Spirit, and we will consider the one big thing he does.

In chapter 2 you will discover how you can experience the supernatural presence of the Holy Spirit every day, every hour, every moment of your life.

In chapter 3 we will talk about what it means to be filled with the Holy Spirit, a supernatural experience that depends on your willingness to surrender to his control. You will find out what it means to walk in the Spirit and produce the fruit of the Spirit in your life.

Chapter 4 is all about the supernatural understanding the Holy Spirit gives you, especially when it comes to deciphering and applying the spiritual truths and principles found in God's written Word, the Bible. But it doesn't stop there. You will also discover how the Holy Spirit helps you in your conversations, whether they are with other people or with God.

The gifts of the Holy Spirit are detailed in chapter 5. You will find that every Christian has at least one gift distributed by the Holy Spirit to be used in service for God and his church.

Chapter 6 gets to the heart of what it means to be empowered by the Holy Spirit. You may be surprised to learn that the expression of this power is different from what you think or what other people may have told you.

Finally, in chapter 7 we will get down in the trenches and dig into the depths of understanding how the Holy Spirit helps you when you experience brokenness and pain.

My prayer for you is the same as the one the apostle Paul prayed for the church in Ephesus:

> *I pray that out of his glorious riches he may strengthen you with power through his Spirit in your inner being, so that Christ may dwell in your hearts through faith. And I pray that you, being rooted and established in love, may have power, together with all the Lord's holy people, to grasp how wide and long and high and deep is the love of Christ, and to know this love that surpasses knowledge—that you may be filled to the measure of all the fullness of God* (Ephesians 3:16-19 NIV).

ONE MORE THING
BEFORE WE GET STARTED

Actually, two more things: fire and wind. After all, these two "elements" form the title of this book. I didn't give the book this title because I am some superspiritual charismatic person with special insights and powers. This is the title because fire and wind comprise two of the core descriptions the Bible uses to give us insights into the power and presence of the Holy Spirit.

Fire is one of the most powerful elements in the natural world. In ancient times fire was an object of superstition and awe. Even today, long after science has harnessed fire for practical use, a raging inferno can leave us awestruck.

God has always acknowledged fire as a symbol of his transcendent glory. Where the Holy Spirit is concerned, fire represents the power God gives us and uses for his purposes. Just as science transforms the power of fire and electricity into useful energy, God transforms us into people he can use through the power of the Holy Spirit.

> You will receive power when the Holy Spirit comes upon you. And you will be my witnesses, telling people about me everywhere—in Jerusalem, throughout Judea, in Samaria, and to the ends of the earth (Acts 1:8).

Wind gives us a dynamic picture of the presence of the Holy Spirit. Just as the air we breathe brings us life, the Holy Spirit gives us the very breath of life for our spirit, soul, and body. In Genesis 2:7 we learn that God formed man from the dust and breathed into him the breath of life. In the Gospel of John, Jesus explains it this way:

> The wind blows wherever it pleases. You hear its sound, but you cannot tell where it comes from or where it is going. So it is with everyone born of the Spirit (3:8 NIV).

Fire and wind. Let these striking and beautiful images guide your heart, soul, mind, and strength as you begin your journey into the power and presence of the Holy Spirit.

> His symbols are flame and wind... Fire and tornado are his twin eagles. The spirit swoops into our dull, flat earthbound philosophies as a wind-driven fire that keeps our faith from being dead and our confessions from being lifeless (Calvin Miller).[7]

CHAPTER 1

Who Is the Holy Spirit?

God made you for something more. You may be living a satisfying life, but there's more to this life than being satisfied. To be clear, there's nothing wrong with having the essentials of life covered: experiencing meaningful relationships, making a living, planning for the future, and being happy. All of these can be satisfying, but none of them are the goal, the secret, the key to a meaningful life.

That's because at some point relationships sour, the job doesn't go well, and the future doesn't turn out the way we envision. As for happiness, well, that depends on circumstances, and as we all know, circumstances are pretty much outside our control. So there has to be something more, something outside ourselves that brings more than mere satisfaction.

My own story has *satisfaction* written all over it. I grew up in a home where God was a part of everyday life. I knew God from an early age, and my parents were consistent in how they lived. They volunteered for important jobs in our little church (my dad served on the church board, and my mom was the choir director), and we attended both Sunday night and Wednesday night services. But even with all my exposure to church and other Christians, rarely—if ever—did I experience the abundant life the Bible talks about.

Oh, I had my spiritual advantages. Among them was being part of a nurturing network of Christian uncles, aunts, and cousins who kept me from straying off the "straight and narrow" through my middle- and high-school years. I also went to a Christian camp for a week every summer. After graduation, I attended a Christian college where I learned about the Bible and met my future wife, Karin.

After we were married, Karin and I were asked by our pastor to lead a class of young married couples using the book *Communication: Key to Your Marriage* by H. Norman Wright (a great book that's still in print, by the way). We said yes, and that started a pattern of leading or being involved in book and Bible studies with other couples for pretty much our entire married life.

I've had the spiritual basics covered, and I am grateful to God and the people who love me that my life as a Christian has been, for the most part, satisfying. But until recently it's not been particularly meaningful. I didn't know why, but that's the way it was. Until I discovered that box in my attic.

WHAT I WAS MISSING

What I haven't shared with you is that my father died when he was just 26 years old. I was four. Because he was sick for the last two years of his life, I really didn't know him. I have slivers of memory that replay in my head from time to time, but I didn't know him like a child knows a father. Over the years I have pieced together bits of his personality from his brother and sisters, but that kind of information didn't help me know the person he really was—his ambitions and beliefs, his hopes and dreams. I had no idea if he believed his life to be meaningful or merely satisfying.

The box of books I discovered a year ago has helped me know my father better. For one thing, I was surprised (shocked?) that my father, raised in a conservative Christian home in a Mennonite community in Minnesota, was focused on the Holy Spirit. Mom never told me this. A few years after my father died, she married a wonderful man who adopted me as his son. My new dad had also been raised in a Mennonite community, and when he married my mother and adopted me, the three of us attended a conservative, Bible-teaching church in central California—the church where I learned about Jesus and the Bible and how to live the Christian life.

My knowledge of the Holy Spirit came primarily from a large Pentecostal church in our town, but not because I ever attended. I based my information on rumors and innuendo. Once in a while we would hear about people in that church doing some things that were unfamiliar to me, such as speaking in tongues and healing people. I didn't necessarily attribute those unusual activities to the Holy Spirit. Actually, I didn't think about them much, because they were so foreign to my own spiritual upbringing. If I had an opinion about Pentecostal or charismatic people, it was that I thought they relied too much on emotion.

My experience at Bible college didn't change that perception. I received a solid, biblically based education, but the Holy Spirit was mentioned only in the context of Bible "doctrine," studying the beliefs of the church based on an understanding of Scripture developed over the centuries. I had no concept of the Holy Spirit's power and presence. I knew *about* the Holy Spirit, but I didn't *know* him.

I had no idea how much I was missing.

Knowing certain doctrinal points about God is an important and necessary part of the Christian life, but that's where I stopped. And that's where I was missing out. "Doctrine explains *who* the Holy Spirit is," writes Tozer. "The next step is to fellowship with and experience the Holy Spirit in ways that cannot be explained in human terms."[1]

That unexplainable experience comes when we allow the Holy Spirit to breathe into us so we can have abundant life and energy. As Simpson writes, "He brings to us the very breath of life for spirit, soul, and body, and creates the atmosphere in which we see the things of God, hear His voice, and dwell in the warmth and radiance of His love."[2]

Torrey reflects on the glorious thought that the Holy Spirit has come into our hearts to make his home there, to "take possession of our lives and make use of them."

> I can think of no thought more humbling or more overwhelming than the thought that a person of divine majesty and glory dwells in my heart and is ready to use even me.[3]

It's not intellectual knowledge (something I'm pretty good at grasping), but "sensible" or "felt" knowledge that comes through an acute awareness of the third Person of the Holy Trinity. For most of my life I lived without an awareness on any level of the immediacy of God in my life. My knowledge was objective, not "felt." Consequently, my relationship with God (and, by association, Jesus and the Holy Spirit) was objective and void of any feeling.

By God's grace, I have come to know the Holy Spirit in an entirely new way, and that's what I want to share with you.

THE BREATH OF GOD

The Holy Spirit is as essential for living the Christian life as oxygen is to the air we breathe. In fact, the Holy Spirit is compared to wind. In a nighttime encounter with a Jewish leader, Jesus said, "The wind blows where it wishes, and you hear its sound, but you do not know where it comes from or where it goes. So it is with everyone who is born of the Spirit" (John 3:8 esv).

For most of my life I thought this meant the Holy Spirit whooshes around me through other, more spiritual people who know how to pray with great passion, who talk about the way God leads them, and who always have a story to tell about the Holy Spirit's power and "anointing." But I never thought that applied to me. I'm ashamed to admit it now, but I didn't think I needed the Holy Spirit. My spiritual vitality was found in the Bible.

Consequently, it was important for me to study the Bible so I could have the kind of experience I perceived others as having. Only it didn't work out that way. The more I studied, the more knowledge I accumulated. But I didn't feel closer to God. As for the Holy Spirit, I knew *about* him, but I didn't *know* him.

MORE THAN DOCTRINE

How much I was missing! Bible knowledge and doctrine are a necessary part of the Christian life, just as mathematical equations and observations about nature are a necessary part of being a scientist. But unless scientists experience what they are studying, they won't fully know and appreciate the natural world. In the same way, unless Christians experience what they are studying, they won't fully know and appreciate the supernatural world.

Remember what Tozer said: "Doctrine explains *who* the Holy Spirit is. The next step is to fellowship with and experience the Holy Spirit in ways that cannot be explained in human terms."[4] As best as I can tell, that inexpressible experience comes when we allow the Holy Spirit to breathe into us.

The thing is, because I am human, God has already "breathed into" me. The Bible says, "God formed the man of dust from the ground and breathed into his nostrils the breath of life" (Genesis 2:7 ESV). In one of the oldest books of the Bible, Elihu captures this picture of the Spirit's power to give life: "The Spirit of God has made me, and the breath of the Almighty gives me life" (Job 33:4 ESV). Another of Job's so-called "friends" also noticed a spiritual presence: "A spirit glided past my face," whispered Eliphaz, "and the hair on my body stood on end" (4:15 NIV).

Have you ever experienced something like that? In a moment of wonder and awe and perhaps fear, have you felt the presence of something you couldn't explain? Do not discount that with a shudder. Did you ever consider that it may have been the breath of God, as real to you as anything you have experienced?

What a beautiful image of what the Holy Spirit does for

us. This isn't some distant reality meant only for a few people. The experience of living in the grace and power of the Holy Spirit is what Gordon Smith calls "immediate." So many things we wish to have are far off, and sometimes it's a struggle to get them. For example, we may want a healthier body, a certain athletic skill, or enough smarts to pass the bar. The time it takes to meet these goals often overwhelms us, so much so that it's easier to give up than to pursue them.

The experience of the Holy Spirit isn't like that. There's no ramp up. You aren't required to gain a certain level of knowledge so you can pass some theological exam. The experience of the Holy Spirit doesn't depend on intellectual knowledge, but on felt knowledge that comes through an awareness of the third Person of the Holy Trinity. The problem is that many Christians live without this awareness of the immediacy of God in their lives. That was me! I knew *about* the Holy Spirit, but I didn't *know* him.

WHAT IS A SPIRITUAL LIFE?

One of the reasons I have been reluctant to embrace felt knowledge is because I have connected it to *uninformed* knowledge. I incorrectly thought that the people who talked about the Holy Spirit in terms of feeling rather than knowing didn't care about Bible doctrine. I suppose there is some of that going on, but so what? I can't be responsible for what others know or don't know. Besides, isn't it just as bad to have a head full of knowledge about the Holy Spirit while failing to have a heart for him?

The truth is, it isn't either-or, but both-and. You need to know *about* the Holy Spirit, and you need to *know* him. I started with the head knowledge first, but I suppose it's quite possible to know the Holy Spirit before knowing about him. Since I didn't grow up in a Pentecostal tradition, my perspective may appear to show just one side of this knowledge business. So let's deal with this before moving on.

There's no shortcut to knowing the Holy Spirit, just as there's no shortcut to knowing God or Jesus. If it takes time for us to get to know ordinary people we can see, what makes us think we can speed date the Holy Spirit and know all there is to know simply by feeling his presence?

Still, the Pentecostal movement over the last 100 years has done the spiritual world a favor by its emphasis on the *immediacy* (to use Gordon Smith's word) of the spiritual world. Where the Holy Spirit dwells is not "out there" somewhere, but right in front of you. Or, to be even more biblical and accurate, it's right there *inside* you.

In the church tradition I grew up with and have been part of, just the opposite is taught. To be spiritual, you need to perform—attend church, read your Bible faithfully, pray a lot, teach a Sunday school class, take mission trips, and put something in the offering plate. All good things, but they do nothing in and of themselves to make you more spiritual. The only value these "good works" have is when they naturally flow out of a life that is spiritual.

God wants us to be spiritual because he wants us to see everything and do everything from his perspective. That's because "God is Spirit, so those who worship him must worship in spirit and in truth" (John 4:24). But becoming spiritual on our own by doing good works is impossible. We need help, and that's where the Holy Spirit comes in.

The apostle Paul writes in his letter to the Romans, "All

who are led by the Spirit of God are children of God" (8:14). A truly spiritual person is someone who is personally led by God through the Holy Spirit. As Torrey puts it, "A true Christian life is not one governed by a long set of rules without us, but led by a living and ever-present person within us."⁵ The Holy Spirit's function in the life of the believer is to help us become spiritually minded in everything we do so that two things will happen: We will see the world from God's perspective, and the world will see God's perspective in us.

WHO IS THE HOLY SPIRIT?

We've been talking about the Holy Spirit as fire and wind, which is entirely appropriate. But before we continue our exploration of the power and presence of the Holy Spirit, I want to direct your attention to the Holy Spirit as a *Person*, beginning with how he fits into the idea of the three-in-one God, commonly known as the Trinity.

No matter how old you are or how mature you are as a Christian, the Trinity is not an easy concept to comprehend. When our children were young, my wife and I bought a book for them that used the apple as the "core" illustration for understanding the Trinity, mainly because an apple has three parts: the core, the flesh, and the skin. One fruit, three parts. Seems simple enough, even to a four-year-old, and I would not deter any parent from explaining the Holy Trinity in this way. But for those of us who want to understand the Trinity in a way that reveals the truth about who God, Jesus, and the Holy Spirit really are and how they relate to one another, we have to look beyond apples.

Yes, there are three parts to an apple, but each "part" is

independent of the others, and each part isn't the entire apple. If someone gave you just the peeled skin of an apple, you wouldn't say, "What a fine-looking apple." You would more likely make a face and say, "Where's the rest of the apple?"

By comparison, when you encounter God, you don't ask, "Where's the rest of you?" Jesus told his disciples, "Anyone who has seen me has seen the Father" (John 14:9 NIV). The people who saw Jesus face-to-face saw all of God, not just a part of God. In exactly the same way, when you consider the Holy Spirit, you will never wonder, "Where's the rest of God?"

The mystery and beauty of the Trinity is that we can know God because he has revealed himself through his three Persons: God the Father, God the Son, and God the Holy Spirit. When we receive the free gift of salvation authored by God, accomplished by Jesus, and applied by the Holy Spirit, we enter into a relationship with all three.

"What this means is that we always have communion with God—not a part of God," writes Tim Chester. "If I have communion with the Son, then I have communion with the Father and the Spirit. The Spirit is the Spirit of God and the Spirit of Christ. So to be in-dwelt by the Spirit is to be in-dwelt by the Son and the Father."[6]

JESUS HAD TO GO SO THE HOLY SPIRIT COULD COME

Jesus came as the divine presence in human form. He related to people on the deepest level—more so than any person who ever walked the earth. When Jesus asked his closest disciples if they wanted to leave him when others decided to no longer follow him, Simon Peter answered, "Lord, to whom would we go? You have the words that give eternal life. We believe, and we know you are the Holy One of God" (John 6:68-69).

We can only imagine the surprise and shock the disciples felt when Jesus told them he was going to leave them. During a meal on the night Jesus was betrayed, he was clear that his departure was imminent. But he told them it would be a good thing for one simple reason: When he left, the Holy Spirit would come. "In fact, it is best for you that I go away," Jesus told them, "because if I don't, the Advocate won't come. If I do go away, then I will send him to you" (John 16:7).

This name, Advocate, has the meaning of "counselor," like an attorney pleading or presenting a case. Catherine Marshall preferred the name Helper to describe what the Holy Spirit does for us. I like all of these descriptions. It reinforces the reality that the Holy Spirit is a Person and not some impersonal force. Marshall agrees. "The Helper is no influence; he is rather a Person—one of three Persons of the Godhead. As such, he possesses all the attributes of personality."[7]

When you are with a person, you are in the *presence* of that person. That's the way the disciples felt when they were with Jesus. They were in his presence. They heard his voice and observed his actions firsthand, including the miracles he performed. But Jesus could only be with them when he was *with* them. After Jesus ascended into heaven, the Holy Spirit became then, and continues to be, the presence of Jesus in us. Even more, the Holy Spirit is the presence of the Trinity— Father, Son, and Holy Spirit—in us and among us.

Jesus told his disciples that he would not abandon them "as orphans" (John 14:18). He assured them that he would come to them. And the way he would do that was by asking the Father to give them "another Advocate" who would never leave them (verse 16).

Now, to be clear, the Holy Spirit was already in the world, but he was not yet a presence in the life of every person who believed in Jesus. All that would change when Jesus ascended into heaven 40 days after his resurrection (Acts 1:9-11)—where he is now, seated at the right hand of the Father (Hebrews 10:12). And from that place in heaven Jesus continues to work through all who trust in him by means of the Holy Spirit.

THE TRINITY'S GIFT

"God is in the Spirit who comes to us, even as He was in the Son," writes Murray. "The gift of the Spirit is the most personal act of the Godhead. It is the gift of Himself to us."[8]

This gift of the Trinity was wonderfully and powerfully revealed when Jesus rose into heaven. As Jesus ascended, the Holy Spirit descended, bringing the power and presence of God to all who believe in Jesus. In the following passage from Paul's letter to the church in Rome, notice how freely Paul moves between the Spirit of God and the Spirit of Christ. They are distinct, yet one and the same—dwelling in us, giving us power and life and the ability to be controlled by God.

> You are not controlled by your sinful nature. You are controlled by the Spirit if you have the Spirit of God living in you. (And remember that those who do not have the Spirit of Christ living in them do not belong to him at all.) And Christ

> lives within you, so even though your body will
> die because of sin, the Spirit gives you life because
> you have been made right with God. The Spirit of
> God, who raised Jesus from the dead, lives in you.
> And just as God raised Christ Jesus from the dead,
> he will give life to your mortal bodies by this same
> Spirit living within you (Romans 8:9-11).

There is a tendency to treat the Holy Spirit like something "other" that we can use when needed. But the Holy Spirit isn't an object. He isn't a commodity, something you can acquire by saying some magic words or mustering up a certain quantity of faith. You can't earn the Holy Spirit. He's not a prize, a force, an influence, or some kind of spiritual vitamin boost. The Holy Spirit isn't a good luck charm.

The Holy Spirit dwelling in you is a divine Person, the third member of the Holy Trinity. The Holy Spirit is God—all-powerful, all-knowing, inhabiting the depth and height and breadth of the universe. He was involved in creating the world, yet he existed before and beyond anything that was made.

The Holy Spirit has intellect. He "searches out everything" and reveals "God's deep secrets" (1 Corinthians 2:10). He exists everywhere, in every dimension, so that those who know him are ever in his presence (Psalm 139:7). The Holy Spirit has emotions. He loves (Romans 15:30), has a will (Acts 16:6), and expresses sorrow (Ephesians 4:30).

> [The Holy Spirit is] a real person, just as real as
> Jesus Christ Himself, an ever-present, loving
> friend and mighty helper, who is not only always
> by their side but dwells in their heart every day

and every hour, and who is ready to undertake for them in every emergency of life.[9]

SENT BY THE
FATHER AND SON

If there's a single Bible verse that everyone knows, it's John 3:16: "God so loved the world that he gave his one and only Son, that whoever believes in him shall not perish but have eternal life" (NIV). This is Jesus speaking to Nicodemus (a Pharisee who came to him at night), explaining how it's possible for a human to be "born again." The next verse expands this thought of God sending Jesus so that we might be saved: "God did not send his Son into the world to condemn the world, but to save the world through him" (verse 17 NIV).

God sent Jesus to earth in real time and space to inhabit a real human body—to live a perfect life, to die and rise from the dead—so that anyone who believes in him will be saved. Thirty-three years after his birth, Jesus explained to his disciples that after he returned to heaven, God would send the Holy Spirit to inhabit those who believe in his Son (John 14:16-17). Later that same evening, once again talking about the Holy Spirit, Jesus told them, "I will send him to you" (John 16:7 NIV).

This has always confused me just a bit. Who sent the Holy Spirit: God or Jesus? Who gave us this supernatural gift? The answer is both. As one of the ancient creeds states,

> I believe in the Holy Spirit, the Lord, the giver of life,
> who proceeds from the Father and the Son,

who with the Father and the Son is adored and glorified.[10]

But there's more! Not only did the Father and the Son send the Holy Spirit as a special gift, but the Spirit freely gives himself in the form of spiritual gifts that are distributed to each and every Christian. (We'll talk more about spiritual gifts in chapter 5.)

The apostle Paul expresses this truth in beautiful language to the early church in Galatia:

> When the right time came, God sent his Son, born of a woman, subject to the law. God sent him to buy freedom for us who were slaves to the law, so that he could adopt us as his very own children. And because we are his children, God has sent the Spirit of his Son into our hearts, prompting us to call out, "Abba, Father." Now you are no longer a slave but God's own child. And since you are his child, God has made you his heir (Galatians 4:4-7).

This is an astounding reality. Because the Spirit of Christ dwells in our hearts, we can call God by his most intimate name, "Abba, Father." Only one other person in the New Testament calls on God this way. When Jesus was in deep and sorrowful prayer in the Garden of Gethsemane, he cried out to God, saying, "Abba, Father," as he was about to experience the agony of the cross (Mark 14:36).

Let this truth wash over you. Because you have the indwelling Spirit of Christ, you have the same intimate access to

God the Father that Jesus has. No matter what you are going through, regardless of the depth of your pain and sorrow, you can cry out to God with the same passion and intensity that Jesus did. This is why Paul can write,

> You have not received a spirit that makes you fearful slaves. Instead, you received God's Spirit when he adopted you as his own children. Now we call him, "Abba, Father." For his Spirit joins with our spirit to affirm that we are God's children (Romans 8:15-16).

THE SPIRIT OF CHRIST

For most of my Christian life I have believed that it is Christ who lives in me—and that's true. Paul writes, "My old self has been crucified with Christ. It is no longer I who live, but Christ lives in me. So I live in this earthly body by trusting in the Son of God, who loved me and gave himself for me" (Galatians 2:20).

We talk about inviting Jesus into our hearts, and that's fine. God is fine with it. Jesus is fine with it. The Holy Spirit is especially fine with it. Because it is the work of the Holy Spirit to reveal Christ to us. Speaking of the Holy Spirit, Jesus told his disciples in that upper room, "He will bring me glory by telling you whatever he receives from me" (John 16:14). Furthermore, it is the work of the Holy Spirit to "testify" about Jesus (see John 15:26)—that is, to be a witness for Jesus to all people. That's why he is called "the Spirit of Christ."

"But there is a deeper reason why the Holy Spirit is called

'the Spirit of Christ,' " writes Torrey, "namely, because it is the work of the Holy Spirit to reveal Christ to us." He continues,

> Just as the Holy Spirit literally and physically formed Jesus Christ in the womb of the Virgin Mary (Luke 1:35), so the Holy Spirit spiritually but really forms Jesus Christ within our hearts today.

Torrey is simply echoing the apostle Paul, who prayed that God would empower believers "with inner strength through his Spirit," so that "Christ will make his home in your hearts as you trust in him" (Ephesians 3:16-17). Torrey concludes,

> It is the privilege of every believer in Christ to have the living Christ formed by the power of the Holy Spirit in his own heart, and therefore the Holy Spirit who thus forms Christ within the heart is called the Spirit of Christ.[11]

THE ONE BIG THING

The Holy Spirit has always been about Jesus. He is equal to God in every way, and yet there is not a more important role for the Holy Spirit than to bring attention to Jesus. That is his one big thing.

The prophet Isaiah said the Spirit would rest upon the Messiah and give him wisdom, understanding, power, and knowledge (Isaiah 11:2). Because he is fully God, Jesus had all of these qualities already, but he chose to obey and depend on the Holy Spirit (verse 3). As a result, the Holy Spirit played a key role in every step and stage of Jesus' life on earth.

The Virgin Birth

The Holy Spirit made possible the "inconceivable" miracle of God coming to earth in human form by being born of a woman (Matthew 1:20).

The Life and Ministry of Jesus

The Holy Spirit filled and directed Jesus (Luke 4:1), and then he anointed him to preach the good news (verse 18).

The Death of Jesus

Not only was the Holy Spirit responsible for the birth of Jesus, but he also played a role in the death of Jesus. "By the power of the eternal Spirit, Christ offered himself to God as a perfect sacrifice for our sins" (Hebrews 9:14).

The Resurrection of Jesus

Each member of the Trinity played a part in the resurrection of Jesus. God the Father raised Jesus from the dead (Ephesians 1:19-20). Jesus had the power to raise himself from the dead (John 10:18). And the Holy Spirit was the means by which God raised Jesus from the dead (Romans 1:4).

This is a book about the power and presence of the Holy Spirit, but as we explore the ways he freely gives us his power and breathes his presence into us, let us always remember that Jesus deserves all glory and honor and praise. Tozer says it well:

> There is a throne, and a man sits on the throne. The man is Jesus Christ the Lord…The Man sitting on that throne is invested with authority, power,

judgment, and justice, so He can wield all authority in heaven and on earth. The man is Jesus Christ the Lord, and the Holy Ghost is here to witness to Him within our hearts. When Jesus spoke, He spoke in the ears of the people, but the Holy Ghost penetrates the heart and speaks in a way that even Jesus could not speak while on the earth.[12]

CHAPTER 2

The Presence of the Holy Spirit

When my father died at such a young age, my mother was shell-shocked. He had been studying for the ministry. She was going to be a pastor's wife. My father and mother probably dreamed of having a lot of children. My father had four siblings, my mother seven. I came along when my parents were in their early twenties. A year and a half later, my sister was born, but she didn't make it past the first day.

"Your baby is in the freezer," the nurse told my mother while she was still recovering from the painful delivery. A week later, as my parents were getting dressed for the memorial service—he in his only suit, she in a plain black dress—my mother noticed my father was struggling to button the collar of his shirt. She tried to help and felt his neck with her fingers. It was swollen. She knew something was wrong. They soon

39

discovered that my father was in the advanced stages of Hodg-kin's disease, a form of cancer called the "young man's disease" at the time. There was no successful treatment. He would be dead in 18 months.

Over the years I have had time to think about those trau-matic events and wonder what it must have been like for this young couple. But at the age of seven, three years after my father passed away in Chicago, I was thinking only of what I was going to do the next day. My mother and I had moved to California, and one night she was driving home after we had had dinner with relatives. It was dark, but the moon was full and bright. In those days a kid could lie on the back seat without a seat belt. That's where I was, looking out the back window of my mother's Ford, staring at the moon and think-ing about things my parents had taught me. About Jesus and my sins and how he was ready to take them away if I would only ask.

I was seven. I didn't feel like a bad person, but that night my thoughts turned to my sins. Not the kind of sins you think about as an adult or even as an older kid, but sins just the same. I looked up at the moon shining bright against the sky. To me it looked otherworldly. The heavenly night turned my thoughts to Jesus and his return. As the moon ducked behind a cloud and then appeared again, it occurred to me that maybe that's what the sky would look like if Jesus were to come back at that moment. As clear as I'm writing this today, I recall my seven-year-old self thinking, *Am I ready?* I wasn't sure.

I wasn't scared, but suddenly I had this sense of being alone, and I didn't like the feeling. I was seven, but I knew I needed Jesus in my heart. "Mommy, I want to accept Jesus," I called out from the darkness of the back seat.

———

Countless times I have thought about that night and my sudden feeling that I needed forgiveness for my sins, that I needed Jesus. I had had no concept of the dramatic, supernatural transformation that occurred in my life the moment I said yes to Jesus. It would take years for me to grow into and fully appreciate the profound step of faith I took with nothing more than a child's prayer. At a simple level, I knew it was real. I just didn't know *why* it was real or *how* it happened. But I know now. Oh, how I know. And it staggers my mind even as it warms my heart.

You see, there's only one explanation for what happened to me that night on the two-lane highway in the foothills of Southern California. The Holy Spirit met me at the level of my need and understanding, and he convicted me. I was seven years old, and he came to me and told me I needed Jesus. Even today, I am amazed at the power and efficacy of the Holy Spirit, to be that precise in enveloping the heart and mind of a child, while never once intruding. Instead, he simultaneously filled me with a sense of loss at the thought of remaining the way I was and a feeling of hope at the thought of trusting him.

THE CONVICTION OF THE HOLY SPIRIT

Perhaps you could tell a similar story. You may have been a child when the Holy Spirit met you at your point of need, or you might have been a teenager or an adult. But you came to the realization that you were a sinner, that you were unable to gain God's favor on your own. You knew you needed Jesus.

That feeling, that knowing, didn't come by accident. The Holy Spirit filled you with conviction and hope just as surely as he filled me.

On the night Jesus was betrayed, in that upper room over a meal with his disciples, Jesus talked a lot about the Holy Spirit. He described him as the Helper, the Counselor, and the Advocate. He also said the Holy Spirit would convict the world of sin.

> When he comes, he will convict the world of its sin, and of God's righteousness, and of the coming judgment. The world's sin is that it refuses to believe in me. Righteousness is available because I go to the Father, and you will see me no more. Judgment will come because the ruler of this world has already been judged (John 16:8-11).

A short time later, after Jesus ascended into heaven and the church was launched with the coming of the Holy Spirit on the day of Pentecost, the apostle Peter preached one of the most famous sermons in history. Luke the physician, the author of Acts, records the response of the crowd:

> When the people heard this, they were cut to the heart and said to Peter and the other apostles, "Brothers, what shall we do?" (Acts 2:37 NIV).

How did this happen? The Holy Spirit had come just as Jesus had promised he would, and in this particular instance he did exactly what Jesus said he would do. He convicted the people listening to Peter's sermon.

"He pricked men to their heart with a sense of their awful

guilt in the rejection of their Lord and their Christ," writes Torrey.[1] That's the King James Version talking. Modern translations, like the New International Version, use the phrase "cut to the heart." Either way, it's a violent image: pricking, cutting, piercing the heart with deep sorrow.

We've softened the convicting work of the Holy Spirit considerably, haven't we? We wait for the Holy Spirit to nudge us, warm us, fill us. We are invited by a pastor or a friend or a book to accept the abundant life Jesus offers, and it's there waiting for us, beckoning us. We think it's an easy, natural decision, but deciding to follow Christ is not easy. And it's definitely not natural. We who have lived in darkness "have seen a great light" (Isaiah 9:2 NIV), but the desire to hang on to our former life is intense. The prince of darkness will not let go easily. The "natural" thing to do is stay the way we are.

The Battle for Our Souls

The truth is that there is a great cosmic battle for our eternal souls. This isn't some poetic image or metaphor. This is real. In order for Jesus to loosen the grip the enemy has on our hearts, he sent the Holy Spirit to convict us—not gently or with a whisper, but with violent agitation so that we, like the people listening to Peter's sermon, have a clear and present sense of our "awful guilt," causing us to cry out, "What shall we do?"

We don't like to talk about guilt, but that's the effect the Holy Spirit has on people. Even at the age of seven, I had a sense of guilt. It worried me to the point of dread: I didn't want Jesus to come that night and pass me by. It was an awful feeling, but it was a feeling I needed because I was committing the greatest sin of all. I was rejecting Christ.

"The world's sin is that it refuses to believe in me," Jesus said (John 16:9). This is the greatest of all sins. We think murder or terrorism or even adultery is the greatest sin. As difficult and disruptive to normal life as those sins are, they do not rise to the eternal implications and consequence of failing to believe in the plan God designed through Jesus to rescue us from darkness and bring us into his glorious light. My seven-year-old, convicted self didn't understand the cosmic scope of what was at stake. I was clueless as to the powers of darkness that gripped my soul. But I knew what to do because the Holy Spirit cut my little heart to the quick.

I thank God that I responded to the Holy Spirit. My prayer was simple, my faith childlike. But the work of God in my heart was no less dramatic than it would have been if I were 30 years older and a hardened criminal who accepted Jesus in prison. Whenever a soul crosses over from the kingdom of darkness into the kingdom of God's glorious light, it's a cause for celebration.

Speaking to a group of "tax collectors and other notorious sinners" (Luke 15:1) who often came to hear him teach, Jesus told the story of the lost sheep, concluding with this truth about the effect of someone coming to saving faith:

> There is more joy in heaven over one lost sinner who repents and returns to God than over ninety-nine others who are righteous and haven't strayed away! (verse 7).

Why the celestial celebration? What's the big deal? Doesn't this happen all the time? Yes, people of all stripes, of all ages, and from all places accept the free gift of salvation every day.

But that shouldn't in any way minimize the supernatural significance of someone responding to the convicting ministry of the Holy Spirit by saying yes to Jesus. The battle for our eternal souls is so fierce and consequential that when we acknowledge our sinful state and surrender our lives to Christ, the good news reaches to the heights of heaven, where great joy erupts. (And I suppose it also reaches to the depths of hell, where I have no doubt there is seething disappointment.)

The power of sin is real. It has such a grip on each of us—whether we're seven or twenty-seven or seventy-seven—that only the power of the cross and the resurrected Christ can overcome it. We think we're good people, especially when we compare ourselves to others. And God loves us, but he's realistic about who we are. Here are some lines from the pen of King David, who understood human nature all too well:

> The LORD looks down from heaven
> on the entire human race;
> he looks to see if anyone is truly wise,
> if anyone seeks God.
> But no, all have turned away;
> all have become corrupt.
> No one does good,
> not a single one! (Psalm 14:2-3).

The only hope we have is for the Holy Spirit to pierce our hearts with the realization of our own sin. And then we have to respond by agreeing with God that we are helpless apart from the saving Person and work of Jesus. You know as well as I do that the world is filled with people who know they need Jesus but refuse to give up the very thing that separates them from a holy God. "Unconfessed sin makes saving faith impossible," writes Tozer. "People struggle to believe mainly because they are hanging on to their sin."[2]

Saying Yes to Jesus Is Not Easy

Just because the Holy Spirit does some surgical piercing in our hearts and consciences doesn't automatically mean we will say yes to Christ. Remorse for the lives we lead is not enough. We still have to acknowledge our sins and ask Jesus to come into our lives.

Tozer observes that "as the Spirit persists, one of two things will happen":

1. "You surrender to his voice, say yes, and believe on His Son actively."

2. "The voice can no longer be heard…You will think the voice is no longer speaking. But it is the death of the heart."[3]

Many years ago I had a good friend who was very successful in business. He was a great person but was not a Christian, although for some reason he liked associating with Christians. I prayed for him frequently, and I know many others were praying as well. We invited him to events where successful people shared their own journeys from sin to surrender, but it seemed that the more we all prayed for our friend, the more hardened to the gospel he became. I have no doubt that the Holy Spirit was convicting him, but he was more comfortable hanging on to his sin than yielding control of his life.

I am so thankful to the depths of my soul that I said yes to the voice of the Holy Spirit when he pierced my heart. "Those who can still feel the sting of the Holy Ghost ought to thank God on their knees," Tozer continues, "for many people's hearts are dead."[4]

It is precisely because of our tendency to hang on to our sin rather than surrender to Jesus that our Savior and the Holy Spirit have a standing offer, inviting us to step from the darkness into the light. In the last chapter of the last book of the Bible, John sees the final in a series of unimaginable visions. It is one of the most tender and beautiful passages in all of Scripture. It shows how the Holy Spirit who convicts and the Savior who brings living water work together to offer this eternal invitation.

> The Spirit and the bride say, "Come." Let anyone who hears this say, "Come." Let anyone who is thirsty come. Let anyone who desires drink freely from the water of life (Revelation 22:17).

THE REGENERATION OF THE HOLY SPIRIT

The process of a sinful person coming to faith in Christ is like a drama unfolding on a stage or screen. You watch the action involving actors and scenery and music, and you get caught up in the story, temporarily forgetting that what you are enjoying is the direct result of many specialists—including a producer and director—working "behind the scenes" to make the play or film realistic and enjoyable.

For me, this metaphor fits the story of salvation. Throughout the years, as I have lived my spiritual life in Christ through the presence and in the power of the Holy Spirit, I have been generally unaware of the supernatural activities going on "behind the scenes" on my behalf. But now, when I think about what it took to bring me to this place, how deeply every member of the Trinity is involved…when I contemplate what it cost Almighty God to carry out his plan to save me through the sacrifice of his only Son…when I reflect on how much the Father, Son, and Holy Spirit are doing for me now…when I consider all God has done and continues to do for me…how can I not be utterly awed and humbled and grateful?

The convicting power of the Holy Spirit is one of those hidden factors that brought me to saving faith. The next is regeneration, the "behind the scenes" supernatural activity on my behalf to bring me from darkness to light, from lost to found, from being God's enemy to being God's friend. Tozer's summary of the Christian life is arresting:

> If you are a Christian, you are a miracle and something odd to the world around you… The Christian is one who has been changed by the bestowal of the gift of God: eternal life in the Spirit. He belongs to a different race altogether.[5]

Regeneration in a spiritual sense is exactly the same as regeneration in the biological sense—it has to do with the "restoration or new growth…of organs, tissues, etc. that have been lost, removed, or injured."[6] In his letter to the church at Ephesus, Paul articulated what this looks like in the life of the regenerated Christian:

> Once you were dead because of your disobedience and your many sins. But God is so rich in mercy,

> and he loved us so much, that even though we
> were dead because of our sins, he gave us life when
> he raised Christ from the dead (Ephesians 2:1,4-5).

For too long I have underappreciated the regenerating work of the Holy Spirit. Perhaps I didn't take the sins of my natural self seriously enough. Not that I need to continue to beat myself up over my transgressions, but I need to be aware of what it took to forgive my sins.

Or maybe I have not understood how much goes on "behind the scenes" to bring about my regeneration. The following passage from Paul's letter to Titus, his protégé in the faith, confirms that each member of the Trinity was involved in my salvation. Watch how the Father, Son, and Holy Spirit work together so that we can be heirs of God's salvation, giving us the hope of eternal life.

> At one time we too were foolish, disobedient,
> deceived and enslaved by all kinds of passions
> and pleasures. We lived in malice and envy, being
> hated and hating one another. But when the kind-
> ness and love of God our Savior appeared, he saved
> us, not because of righteous things we had done,
> but because of his mercy. He saved us through the
> washing of rebirth and renewal by the Holy Spirit,
> whom he poured out on us generously through
> Jesus Christ our Savior, so that, having been jus-
> tified by his grace, we might become heirs having
> the hope of eternal life (Titus 3:3-7 NIV).

Simply put, the Holy Spirit makes us Christians because of his regenerating work through "the washing of rebirth and renewal."

The Wind and Breath of God

How does this work? How does the Holy Spirit bring us from spiritual death to spiritual life? This is how Jesus explained it to Nicodemus:

> I assure you, no one can enter the Kingdom of God without being born of water and the Spirit. Humans can reproduce only human life, but the Holy Spirit gives birth to spiritual life. So don't be surprised when I say, "You must be born again." The wind blows wherever it wants. Just as you can hear the wind but can't tell where it comes from or where it is going, so you can't explain how people are born of the Spirit (John 3:5-8).

The Holy Spirit is the wind that blows, the breath of God that breathes new life into our dead lives. Oh, the beauty and mystery of this supernatural reality! The Old Testament prophet Ezekiel was given a vision by God to illustrate this incredible process. There's no Hollywood movie or Netflix series that could possibly match the drama of this scene.

> The LORD took hold of me, and I was carried away by the Spirit of the LORD to a valley filled with bones. He led me all around among the bones that covered the valley floor. They were scattered everywhere across the ground and were completely dried out. Then he asked me, "Son of man, can these bones become living people again?"
>
> "O Sovereign LORD," I replied, "you alone know the answer to that."

Then he said to me, "Speak a prophetic message to these bones and say, 'Dry bones, listen to the word of the Lord! This is what the Sovereign Lord says: Look! I am going to put breath into you and make you live again! I will put flesh and muscles on you and cover you with skin. I will put breath into you, and you will come to life. Then you will know that I am the Lord.'"

So I spoke this message, just as he told me. Suddenly as I spoke, there was a rattling noise all across the valley. The bones of each body came together and attached themselves as complete skeletons. Then as I watched, muscles and flesh formed over the bones. Then skin formed to cover their bodies, but they still had no breath in them.

Then he said to me, "Speak a prophetic message to the winds, son of man. Speak a prophetic message and say, 'This is what the Sovereign Lord says: Come, O breath, from the four winds! Breathe into these dead bodies so they may live again.'"

So I spoke the message as he commanded me, and breath came into their bodies. They all came to life and stood up on their feet—a great army (Ezekiel 37:1-10).

The immediate application of this prophecy is to the nation of Israel, which was in a depressed and decrepit condition at the time of this prophecy. The people recognized their ruined state and said, "We have become old, dry bones—all hope is gone" (verse 11).

Doesn't that also apply to anyone who knows they are dead in their sins and separated from God? Just as God promised Israel, he promises to breathe life into us "from the four winds." This is the Holy Spirit, who is the eternal life giver, dwelling in every part of the earth, able to reach every hopeless person who cries out for help.

In ancient times, Elihu recognized the life-giving power of the Holy Spirit, even before enjoying the benefit of the written Word of God. "The Spirit of God has made me, and the breath of the Almighty gives me life" (Job 33:4).

When I recognize the Holy Spirit as the wind and breath of God giving me new life, a beautiful unity emerges in my mind. Everything the Holy Spirit touches gives life.

The Holy Spirit was present at creation, "hovering over the surface of the waters" (Genesis 1:2). God "merely spoke, and the heavens were created," writes the psalmist (Psalm 33:6).

The Holy Spirit was present when God created humanity in his image. "The Lord God formed the man from the dust of the ground. He breathed the breath of life into the man's nostrils, and the man became a living person" (Genesis 2:7).

Knowing we need a guide to understand who God is, what he has done for us, and how we can be reconciled to him, he gave us his written Word by the breath of the Holy Spirit. "All Scripture is breathed out by God and profitable for teaching, for reproof, for correction, and for training in righteousness" (2 Timothy 3:16 esv).

When Jesus appeared to his disciples after his resurrection, he breathed on them and told them, "Receive the Holy Spirit" (John 20:22).

THE INDWELLING
OF THE HOLY SPIRIT

The result of spiritual regeneration is nothing short of a miracle. It's the complete transformation of a broken, dead life into a new life. It's the supernatural process of becoming a new person.

> This means that anyone who belongs to Christ has become a new person. The old life is gone; a new life has begun! (2 Corinthians 5:17).

When the Holy Spirit gives us this new life, he doesn't just blow into us and then step back. The Holy Spirit indwells— lives inside—every believer. At the moment of regeneration, the Holy Spirit literally moves in, and suddenly, miraculously, our hearts, souls, minds, and bodies become a dwelling place for the Holy Spirit.

> Don't you realize that your body is the temple of the Holy Spirit, who lives in you and was given to you by God? (1 Corinthians 6:19).

Torrey reflects on this remarkable spiritual reality:

> If we are children of God, we are not so much to pray that the Spirit may come and dwell in us, for He does that already. We are rather to recognize His presence, His gracious and glorious indwelling, and give to Him complete control of the house He already inhabits, and strive so to live as not to grieve this holy one, this divine guest.[7]

Can you see why my new understanding and appreciation of the Holy Spirit's role in my life has energized my spiritual walk with Jesus? I regret that I have underappreciated and perhaps even trivialized the role of the Holy Spirit—indeed, the role of every Person of the Trinity—in my salvation and spiritual life here on earth. But now, as the Holy Spirit has opened the eyes of my heart to his work in my life, I find myself uttering outbursts of gratitude and joy (not necessarily within earshot of others, but definitely so God can hear).

And still there's more. Not only does the Holy Spirit create, convict, regenerate, and indwell us—he also baptizes us.

THE BAPTISM OF
THE HOLY SPIRIT

Now, I will admit that baptism has always been a bit confusing for me. In addition to the sacrament of baptism, which all believers are invited to experience, there seem to be two baptisms of the Holy Spirit. The way you view these baptisms depends on your church tradition. In my tradition (both in the church and at the Christian college I attended), there is just one baptism, a once-for-all process that places all who accept Christ into the body of Christ. (I'm going to talk about that baptism in a minute.)

The other baptism is what is commonly referred to in the Pentecostal tradition as the "second baptism" or "second blessing" of the Holy Spirit, an important and challenging topic we will discuss in chapter 6.

So what is the "first baptism" of the Holy Spirit? Quite simply (but very profoundly) it describes the Holy Spirit's role in bringing all believers together as part of the body of Christ.

What distinguishes baptism from indwelling is this: By his indwelling, the Holy Spirit becomes a part of your life. By the baptism of the Holy Spirit, you become part of the life of the body of Christ.

> We have all been baptized into one body by one Spirit, and we all share the same Spirit (1 Corinthians 12:13).
>
> Don't you realize that all of you together are the temple of God and that the Spirit of God lives in you? (1 Corinthians 3:16).

Not only is the Holy Spirit found in us individually, but he also dwells in the collective body of Christ known as the church, which is comprised of all believers in Jesus Christ, regardless of time and location. That's what Jesus meant when he said, "Where two or three gather together as my followers, I am there among them" (Matthew 18:20). Jesus is present in us both individually and collectively through the presence and power of the Holy Spirit.

> Make every effort to keep yourselves united in the Spirit, binding yourselves together with peace. For there is one body and one Spirit, just as you have been called to one glorious hope for the future. There is one Lord, one faith, one baptism, one God and Father of all, who is over all, in all, and living through all (Ephesians 4:3-6).

The Holy Spirit has given each of us at least one spiritual gift that is to be used within and for the body of Christ (verse

7; read more about that in chapter 5). The Holy Spirit is the member of the Trinity who oversees the administration of the church, each of us working together for the benefit of everyone. This gifting is the direct result of the Spirit's baptism, which is intended to empower Christians for ministry.

> [Christ] makes the whole body fit together perfectly. As each part does its own special work, it helps the other parts grow, so that the whole body is healthy and growing and full of love (Ephesians 4:16).

THE SEAL AND ASSURANCE OF THE HOLY SPIRIT

One of the biggest questions Christians ask about their life with God is this: "How can I be sure I am saved?" This is not an unreasonable question, because becoming a Christian isn't a *transaction*, where you get something tangible in exchange for something you've paid for or earned. Salvation is about *transformation,* and there's no written receipt, mainly because you didn't earn it or pay for it.

Your standing before God, whereby he sees the righteousness of his Son in you, is not based on your effort. The plan of salvation was authored by God, accomplished by Jesus, and applied by the Holy Spirit. It's yours through faith by the grace of God (Ephesians 2:8-9). The transformation is real—as real as anything you will ever experience—but the evidence is ethereal. It's felt, not intellectual, knowledge.

So how do you know you're saved? Once again the Holy Spirit comes to the rescue.

As soon as the Holy Spirit convicts, regenerates, and indwells you, he does something that gives you assurance that the process and effect of your salvation are real. In a word, the Holy Spirit *seals* you.

The word *seal* is full of meaning. It comes primarily from the marketplace. In biblical times, a seal was an official mark showing that a down payment had been made for a piece of property or some other purchase. The seal guaranteed the final payment. "In other words," writes Kelly Kapic, "a part of what will ultimately be given is paid ahead of time as a promise that the last installment will be made."[8]

God has given us the Holy Spirit as that down payment, guaranteeing that the last installment on our eternal inheritance with Jesus Christ will be made.

> When you believed in Christ, he identified you as his own by giving you the Holy Spirit, whom he promised long ago. The Spirit is God's guarantee that he will give us the inheritance he promised and that he has purchased us to be his own people. He did this so we would praise and glorify him (Ephesians 1:13-14).

The Spirit's guarantee is so profound that you can feel it in your soul. He is your inner witness to the transformation that has taken place. This seal is better than anything you could receive in a document because it is given in your heart.

As I look ahead to my eternal life with Christ, I can't help but reflect on my spiritual heritage. My sister passed away when I was two, and my father left this earth when I was four. By God's grace and the Holy Spirit's conviction and regeneration, I said yes to Jesus at the age of seven. Now, decades later, I can reflect on this eternal promise that links my father and sister to me. They haven't been on this earth for some time, but in the blink of an eye I will be in the presence of Jesus and will see my father once again. I will meet my sister for the first time, even as my heavenly Father welcomes me home.

The Holy Spirit guarantees it.

CHAPTER 3

Filled with the Holy Spirit

S omeone should have warned you. Before you signed up for the Christian life, it might have been good to know in advance what you were in for. Rather than entering a life of happiness and bliss, you began to experience struggles and setbacks. You expected fireworks; instead you got discouragement. Not always, but enough to wonder at times what all the hype was about.

Why didn't somebody tell you? You might have reconsidered entering into a relationship with Christ. In fact, had you given the New Testament a thorough reading before you accepted Jesus and were transformed by the Holy Spirit, you would have known what to expect. Just by reading the words of Jesus to his followers, you might have had second thoughts.

> I have told you all this so that you may have peace
> in me. Here on earth you will have many trials
> and sorrows (John 16:33).

> If the world hates you, remember that it hated me
> first. The world would love you as one of its own if
> you belonged to it, but you are no longer part of
> the world. I chose you to come out of the world,
> so it hates you (John 15:18-19).

But you didn't back out. You didn't run. You believed God
and accepted the salvation he authored, Jesus accomplished,
and the Holy Spirit applied. By God's grace and your response
of receiving the free gift of eternal life by faith, you were reborn
and regenerated. You are no longer what you were. You belong
to Jesus Christ and have been changed by him, which means
you have become a new person. Your "old life is gone; a new
life has begun!" (2 Corinthians 5:17). You believed Jesus when
he said, "Take heart, because I have overcome the world"
(John 16:33).

WHY YOU STRUGGLE

Yet you struggle, and I can tell you why. Not because I'm
smarter than you, but because I know what it's like to struggle.
While we have a new life, the old sin nature doesn't go away
after we receive Jesus as Savior and Lord. The apostle Paul
knew about this sin nature all people have, and how it frus-
trates us after we become Christians.

Paul was a by-the-book Jewish leader before his dramatic
conversion. He hunted down and imprisoned Christians,
eager for their execution (see Acts 8:1,3; 9:1-2,13-14). Then,

while Paul was on his way to Damascus to persecute more Christians, Jesus met him in a brilliant flash of light and said to him: "Why are you persecuting me?" (Acts 9:4).

Paul got the message and was transformed from an enemy of Jesus to history's greatest witness for Jesus. He traveled tirelessly, endured persecution of his own, and wrote 13 letters to the churches he planted, sharing his love for Jesus and instructions for living the Christian life. He knew Jesus at a level the rest of us can only aspire to, yet he struggled with sin just like you and me.

> I have discovered this principle of life—that when I want to do what is right, I inevitably do what is wrong. I love God's law with all my heart. But there is another power within me that is at war with my mind. This power makes me a slave to the sin that is still within me (Romans 7:21-23).

Why is this the case? After our conversion, why does our desire to sin continue, especially with the Holy Spirit now indwelling us? In fact, how is it even possible for the Holy Spirit, who is just as much God as Jesus is, to live in the same body as our sin?

As we discovered in the last chapter, our bodies are dwelling places for the Holy Spirit. He is the presence of Christ in us. And because the Holy Spirit is *holy*, he can't tolerate the sin in our lives. So why doesn't the Holy Spirit leave us when we sin? It's quite simple. Without the Holy Spirit, we wouldn't be God's children. Conversely, because we have been born again, the Holy Spirit dwells in us—for good. Paul writes in Romans 8:9:

You are not controlled by your sinful nature. You
are controlled by the Spirit if you have the Spirit
of God living in you. (And remember that those
who do not have the Spirit of Christ living in
them do not belong to him at all.)

YOU ARE A TEMPLE

Paul uses a wonderful metaphor for the Christian life that
helps explain how this works. The metaphor is a temple, or a
place dedicated to the service or worship of a deity. In the Old
Testament, under the Old Covenant, the temple was the dwelling place of God for his chosen people, the Jews. In the New
Testament, under the New Covenant, those who put their
faith in Jesus for salvation become the dwelling place of God.
Under the Old Covenant, the high priest was the intermedi-
ary between a holy God and imperfect people. Under the New
Covenant, our high priest is Jesus.

When God came to earth in human form—the word
incarnation means "God in the flesh"—it was for the purpose
of saving people from their sins. That's the literal meaning of
the name Jesus (Matthew 1:21). The death of Jesus on the cross
was the perfect sacrifice. That's why the prophet John the Baptist cried out these words when he saw Jesus: "Look! The Lamb
of God who takes away the sin of the world!" (John 1:29).

After Jesus was crucified, buried, and resurrected, the old
sacrificial system was no longer needed. At the moment of his
death, the curtain in the temple "was torn in two, from top
to bottom" (Matthew 27:51), announcing rather dramatically
that the old rules were no longer in effect. With the death and
resurrection of Jesus and the coming of the Holy Spirit, people

no longer had to go into the physical temple for the forgiveness of sins.

Each person who accepts the once-for-all sacrifice for sin offered by Jesus becomes the dwelling place of God. He inhabits you in the Person of the Holy Spirit just as surely as he inhabited the temple of the Old Testament. You quite literally become the temple where God dwells. As we have discovered, you also become a habitation for the Holy Spirit and a member of the body of Christ.

> Don't you realize that your body is the temple of the Holy Spirit, who lives in you and was given to you by God? You do not belong to yourself, for God bought you with a high price. So you must honor God with your body (1 Corinthians 6:19-20).

A DWELLING FOR
THE HOLY SPIRIT

On the night he was betrayed, Jesus told his disciples that one of the reasons he was going to leave them was to prepare a place for them in heaven. He described heaven as his Father's house.

> My Father's house has many rooms; if that were not so, would I have told you that I am going there to prepare a place for you? And if I go and prepare a place for you, I will come back and take you to be with me that you also may be where I am (John 14:2-3 NIV).

Before Jesus came to earth, God dwelled in a physical temple. And someday we will dwell with God in his home. In between those two dwellings, God is living in us. We are the physical and spiritual house of Almighty God and his Son, Jesus, because of the presence of the Holy Spirit in us.

This was a revelation for me. I have been a dwelling for the Holy Spirit since I was seven, but I am just now facing and embracing the reality that God is quite literally living in my body—not just in my mind and soul, but also in my heart, in the most literal sense possible. I don't completely understand this supernatural reality, but I accept it, and it fills me with awe and wonder—and sometimes with remorse.

You see, just like the house Jesus is preparing for us in heaven, the house that is my body has many rooms. (I know that's a little hard to grasp, but stay with me.) The Holy Spirit lives in my house, and yet it's possible for me to shove him into a corner because of neglect or lock him in a room because of sin. The Holy Spirit can't be in the same room as my sin, but he won't leave the house. He will just hunker down in the basement or a closet until I do some essential cleaning.

To keep our houses clean is impossible on our own. We need the help of the Holy Spirit to convict us of our sin so we can bring it to Jesus and ask for his forgiveness and cleansing.

> If we confess our sins to him, he is faithful and just to forgive us our sins and to cleanse us from all wickedness (1 John 1:9).

That's what I mean when I say the realization of the Holy Spirit living in me sometimes fills me with remorse. The more I embrace the reality of the presence of the Holy Spirit in my life, the more I am aware that my sin grieves—brings sorrow to—him (Ephesians 4:30).

Do you want to know a little secret? The fact that we struggle with sin and are sometimes filled with remorse for the way we live is a sign that the Holy Spirit dwells in us. Before you were saved, your happiness and pleasure were all that mattered. You were the center of the universe. You did things to please you, and you didn't feel bad about it. But that's your old self. When you surrendered your life to Jesus, you became a new person. And yet from time to time you revert to your old nature and allow self-glorifying enterprises and idols to set up shop in your life. And the Spirit of God just won't put up with it. He wants them cleared out.

You remember the story of Jesus clearing the temple? He was outraged that commercial enterprises had been set up in his Father's house. In a dramatic physical act, he overturned heavy wooden tables and shouted at the people running these nasty little businesses. "The Scriptures declare, 'My Temple will be called a house of prayer,' but you have turned it into a den of thieves!" Jesus said with disdain (Matthew 21:13).

What a startling description of the sin that clogs our houses. Each sin is a thief we've invited into the Holy Spirit's house, and he won't stand for it.

THE FUTILITY
OF FIGHTING SIN

In his letter to the Galatians, Paul lists a sampling of sins that crop up in our lives when we let them in. This is not meant to be an exhaustive list, but it represents the range of attitudes and actions that characterize us when we are in control of our lives.

> When you follow the desires of your sinful nature, the results are very clear: sexual immorality, impurity, lustful pleasures, idolatry, sorcery, hostility, quarreling, jealousy, outbursts of anger, selfish ambition, dissension, division, envy, drunkenness, wild parties, and other sins like these (Galatians 5:19-21).

Paul understands human nature. He knows that when we let the desires that come from our sinful nature control our lives, we are living in conflict with the Spirit who indwells us. We've locked him in the basement, and we're having a party in the living room. We need to unlock the door by clearing out the junk. That means chasing out the bad influences and getting rid of the distractions and temptations.

When I read this list of "evil results" in Galatians, I see them as a fractured reflection of the desires of my sinful nature, like looking in a mirror that's been broken. Granted, I don't have a problem with some of these, but others are all too real.

For all of us, trying to fight these sins one at a time is a losing proposition because we try to do it in the power of the flesh, such as making an effort based on self-discipline or self-improvement. But that just doesn't work because the word *self* is the common denominator.

Fighting our sins and even our benign ambitions is like a game of whack-a-mole. Just when we think we've conquered one, another sin pops up. So we whack that one, and up pops another. It's a futile and frustrating experience because we obsess over our many sins rather than focus on the one God. Here's how Tozer expresses this thought:

> We fall in love with these things and get lost in the plural, whereas God is bringing us slowly to the singular. God is singular: God, the Father; God, the Son; God, the Holy Ghost; the triune God in unity; the three in One. And God is bringing us to this One. We are holding on to the plural, to the many, and forgetting the One.[1]

What's holding us back? What's keeping us from experiencing God's presence and power? Here's my simple take. We are unwilling to give up our meagerness for God's abundance. We are satisfied to have one foot in this world below and one foot in the world above. We're willing to change a little, but God doesn't want our change, our scraps, our leftovers. He wants all of us so we can have all of him.

FILLED WITH THE HOLY SPIRIT

This is what being filled with the Holy Spirit is all about. He already lives in us, so it's not about asking for something that's not there. As we've seen Torrey explain, it's about clearing out the junk so God can have the run of the house. That's what it means to be filled with the Holy Spirit.

> If we are children of God, we are not so much to pray that the Spirit may come and dwell in us, for He does that already. We are rather to recognize His presence, His gracious and glorious indwelling, and give to Him complete control of the house He already inhabits, and strive so to live as not to grieve this holy one, this divine guest.[2]

The indwelling of the Holy Spirit in the life of the believer is a done deal. Once we belong to Christ, there's nothing we can do to undo what God has done for us by putting the Spirit of Christ in us. By comparison, being filled with the Holy Spirit is something we have to initiate. We have to clean house—not just once or once in a while, but every day.

"Be filled with the Holy Spirit," Paul writes (Ephesians 5:18). This isn't a request or a suggestion. It's a command, one that stands in opposition to the first part of the verse: "Don't be drunk with wine." Paul's point is not that we have to give up our favorite cabernet in order to be spiritual. Rather, we need to stop letting our natural inclinations control our lives.

Here are two additional things to note about this filling business. First, even as Christians we tend to default to the desires of our sinful nature because being filled with the Holy Spirit is not easy. Tozer observes:

> To be filled with the Spirit is a most solemn, searching, and sometimes painful experience to go through. The Holy Ghost is not painful. He is the gentle love of God, but getting ourselves ready, getting cleaned up, poured out; confessing, getting forgiven, getting straightened out with people, getting restitutions made, that can be painful.[3]

Second, being filled with the Holy Spirit is by necessity repeatable. Being baptized by the Holy Spirit into the body of Christ is a one-and-done deal. But living in the fullness of the Holy Spirit, where he has control of your life, is an ongoing process. I love Moody's practical advice:

We are leaky vessels, and we have to keep right under the fountain all the time to keep full of Christ... What we want is a fresh supply, a fresh anointing and fresh power, and if we seek it, and seek it with all our hearts, we will obtain it.[4]

LET THE SPIRIT GUIDE YOUR LIFE

So how do we stay fresh? How do we consistently expel our sin and experience the fullness of the Holy Spirit? Our tendency is to try to defeat sin over and over so the Holy Spirit can take control. But that's a frustrating way to live because we focus on the sin when we should be focusing on God. Simpson draws a helpful analogy from nature:

Here is God's great secret of holiness; not fighting sin, but being filled with God. It is the old principle of the expulsive power of a stronger force and a supreme affection. Just as water excludes air from that tumbler when it is filled with water; just as light excludes the darkness when the room is lighted, so the indwelling of the Holy Ghost excludes the presence and power of sin.[5]

Paul explains it like this: "How foolish can you be? After starting your new lives in the Spirit, why are you now trying to become perfect by your own human effort?" (Galatians 3:3). We need to face up to the fact that we can't defeat sin on our own. Only Jesus can help us through the presence and power of the Holy Spirit. We have to make the decision every day and every hour to let the Holy Spirit guide our lives.

I say, let the Holy Spirit guide your lives. Then you won't be doing what your sinful nature craves. The sinful nature wants to do evil, which is just the opposite of what the Spirit wants. And the Spirit gives us desires that are the opposite of what the sinful nature desires. These two forces are constantly fighting each other, so you are not free to carry out your good intentions. But when you are directed by the Spirit, you are not under obligation to the law of Moses (Galatians 5:16-18).

We've already covered the evil results produced by our sinful nature. Now let's look at what happens when we let the Holy Spirit guide our lives.

THE SINGULAR FRUIT OF THE SPIRIT

In contrast to the plurality of our sins is the singularity of the fruit of the Spirit, which flows from a life surrendered to the Holy Spirit. Whereas the sins listed in Galatians 5:19-21 are random and seem to follow no particular pattern, the qualities in Galatians 5:22-23 follow a certain rhyme and reason. There's beauty in their order because they stem from a life lived in the presence and power of the Holy Spirit.

The nine character qualities form a unified whole, giving us a picture of someone living according to their new life in the Holy Spirit. You could say the fruit of the Spirit paints a picture of a true Christian lifestyle. John Stott clusters what he calls "nine Christian graces" into three categories:

- *Love, joy, peace.* These virtues point to our relationship with God. Our first love should be for God, our joy should be in God, and our peace should be with God.

- *Patience, kindness, goodness.* These three virtues refer to our relationship with others. *Patience* is the quality of hanging in there with people, even when they irritate or offend us. *Kindness* reflects a pleasant disposition, and *goodness* emerges from our words and deeds toward others.

- *Faithfulness, gentleness, self-control.* These three virtues focus on our inner selves. When we keep our commitments, we are *faithful.* When we act with humility and an attitude of service, we are *gentle.* And when we exercise *self-control,* we are doing the opposite of gratifying our flesh.[6]

I grew up in the Central Valley of California, which lacks the sophistication of San Francisco to the north and the glamour of Los Angeles to the south. My hometown of Fresno is so boring and ordinary that the city motto is "We live here so you don't have to" (not really, but you get the idea).

The one thing the Central Valley had going for it when I lived there was the fruit grown in its fertile fields. In fact, we liked to boast that our region was the fruit basket of the world. Many of our family members and friends were fruit growers and distributors. Producing fruit was part of the soil and fabric of where I grew up.

If there's one thing I learned after being around so many fruit trees and vines, it's that growing fruit is a slow process.

It can take up to three years for a newly planted vineyard to produce grapes. Same goes for an orange tree. You don't just stick a fruit-bearing plant in the ground and expect it to produce instantly. And then, once the vine or tree begins to produce fruit, that fruit takes time to grow before it is ripe and ready to eat.

Our fruit-bearing lives are no different. The maturing of our character takes time. Fruit bearing is a slow process. The Holy Spirit unites us to Christ—John Calvin said he is "the vital sap" that enables us to bear fruit—and it is only as we abide or remain in him that we will produce the fruit of the Spirit. Jesus explains how this works in his upper room discourse:

> I am the vine; you are the branches. Whoever abides in me and I in him, he it is that bears much fruit, for apart from me you can do nothing. If anyone does not abide in me he is thrown away like a branch and withers; and the branches are gathered, thrown into the fire, and burned. If you abide in me, and my words abide in you, ask whatever you wish, and it will be done for you. By this my Father is glorified, that you bear much fruit and so prove to be my disciples (John 15:5-8 esv).

THE GREATEST IS LOVE

Jesus goes on to explain that a measure of the fruit we are called to bear is the love we have for others, especially other followers of Jesus (verses 9-13). In fact, the one overriding fruit of the Spirit is love. "For all these manifestations of the fruit are but various forms of love," writes Simpson. He demonstrates this through the following list:

> *Joy* is love exulting.
>
> *Peace* is love reposing.
>
> Longsuffering [*patience*] is love enduring.
>
> Meekness [*kindness*] is love with bowed head.
>
> *Goodness* is love in action.
>
> Faith [*faithfulness*] is love confiding.
>
> *Gentleness* is love refined.
>
> Temperance [*self-control*] is true self-love.

"The whole sum of Christian living is just loving," continues Simpson. "And we do not even have to love, but we only have to be filled with the Spirit and then the love will flow as a fountain, spontaneously, from the life within."[7]

BEING FILLED ISN'T A FORMULA

A.W. Tozer was my father's favorite author. I know this because there were more books by Tozer in his box than by any other author. When I open a book by Tozer, I try to imagine what my father would have been thinking, how his heart might have been stirred when he read these words. I can tell you they have a profound effect on me, especially when Tozer warns against treating the filling of the Holy Spirit as a system or formula. It is as much an emotional response as an intellectual one.

> We cannot think our way into the filling of the Spirit. We have to close our eyes and make the leap of faith into the arms of God. After every trick and everything you know to move toward God has failed and your desperate heart cries, "Fill me now, fill me now," then you move into that zone where human reason has to be suspended for a moment and the human heart leaps across into the arms of God. Then human talent and human glory and human honor and human duty and human favor all go out into the darkness of yesterday, and everything is God's honor, God's glory, God's duty, and God's favor. You have been broken and melted before God.[8]

Do you see how this works? In his infinite wisdom, God has engineered a perfect system that brings the glory of God's presence and power—the wind and fire—into the body of Christ and into the inner life of every Christian by the Holy Spirit so we can be the people God wants us to be. "The wind and the fire…are given to enable the church to *be* the church," says N.T. Wright, "in other words, to enable God's people to *be* God's people."

> The Spirit is given so that we ordinary mortals can become, in a measure, what Jesus himself was: part of God's future arriving in the present; a place where heaven and earth meet…The Spirit is given

to begin the work of making God's future real in the present. That is the first, and perhaps the most important, point to grasp about the work of this strange personal power.[9]

CHAPTER 4

The Illumination of the Holy Spirit

I will ask the Father, and he will give you
another Advocate, who will never leave you.
He is the Holy Spirit, who leads into all truth.

JOHN 14:16-17

I made a little joke in the introduction that I grew up in a church and family tradition where the Trinity was composed of the Father, Son, and Holy Bible. In fact, that is the framework that shaped my spiritual life. The Bible has been front and center at the expense of the Holy Spirit. In theory, I have always understood that the Holy Spirit plays an important role in "illuminating" my mind so that I can better know what the Bible means. But on a practical level, my spiritual condition and growth have been inextricably tied to my own efforts to diligently study the Bible.

My reverence for the Bible was initially shaped when, four

years after my father's death, my mother married a man who adopted me and would be my father for the next 43 years. My first father had studied to be a pastor. My adopted father sold books and Bibles to pastors because he owned a Christian bookstore. But not just any Christian bookstore. My family's bookstore was called the Bible House.

That sealed it. From that time forward, the Bible would not only direct my spiritual life, but it would also become the core of my family's livelihood. And it didn't stop there.

Our family of three attended a Bible-teaching church. The pastor of the church I joined when I was in Bible college was a nationally known Bible teacher. After graduation, I got married and returned home to work in the family business, the Bible House.

When I was in my twenties, an older businessman mentored me through a program based on applying the Bible to everyday life. My wife and I began teaching Bible studies to couples and college students, something we have continued to do off and on throughout our married life.

I wouldn't trade any of these experiences and encounters with the Bible for anything. No matter how you read the Bible, there is a benefit. Even the outspoken atheist Richard Dawkins has suggested that people should read the King James Bible, not for its spiritual content, but because it helped shape the English language.

A close family friend had strayed for years from the spiritual path she was walking. And then in a moment of personal crisis she retreated to our family cabin, where her great-grandmother's tattered King James Bible sat on a shelf, dusty and worn. She opened the Bible, started at the beginning (like you do with any book), and read for the better part of 24 hours.

At the end of the weekend, she was a different person. Her encounter with that old King James Bible, illuminated by the Holy Spirit, gave her meaning and direction.

> Whatever God says to us is full of living power: it is sharper than the sharpest dagger, cutting swift and deep into our innermost thoughts and desires with all their parts, exposing us for what we really are (Hebrews 4:12 TLB).

There's that word *cutting* again. That's the Holy Spirit's work. He convicts us by cutting and piercing our hearts, and his surgical work in our lives continues as we read and interact with Scripture.

INSIDE OUT

I think this is where too many of us Bible-believing Christians come up short. We read and study the Bible like it's some kind of textbook, looking for truth and application. We form classes to study books of the Bible. We go to Bible colleges and seminaries in order to learn more about the Bible. All of this activity is good and important and helpful in our spiritual journeys. But the way we approach the Word of God is backward. We treat the Scriptures like a commodity, looking for the benefits. Our reading is structured so that we take in only the parts that appeal to us, avoiding the more difficult sections that end up "exposing us for what we really are." Basically, we center our reading around us.

When we read the Bible this way, we're in charge. And the Holy Spirit, whom God used to breathe his thoughts and intentions and plans for a broken humanity into the original writers, sits in the corner waiting for us to ask him to take the lead in our encounters with Scripture.

Only recently have I started to comprehend just how actively and intimately the Holy Spirit wants to be involved in my Bible reading. For a long time I didn't understand that the Holy Spirit is available to illuminate my mind *in real time,* as I'm reading, so that the Word of God can cut deep into my "innermost thoughts and desires." If I had to do it again, knowing what I am now learning, I would have long ago invited the Holy Spirit to take his proper place in my life as my personal guide and spiritual teacher.

There's a passage in Paul's first letter to the Corinthian church that describes what the Holy Spirit does with God's Word:

> It was to us that God revealed these things by his Spirit. For his Spirit searches out everything and shows us God's deep secrets. No one can know a person's thoughts except that person's own spirit, and no one can know God's thoughts except God's own Spirit... When we tell you these things, we do not use words that come from human wisdom. Instead, we speak words given to us by the Spirit, using the Spirit's words to explain spiritual truths (1 Corinthians 2:10-11,13).

I have read this passage many times, but when I consider it now and think deeply about what it means, it dawns on me that I have been approaching Bible reading and study all wrong. I've been depending on pastors, teachers, books, and commentaries to teach me from the outside in. What I should do is depend on the Holy Spirit to illuminate me from the inside out.

BREATHING IN,
BREATHING OUT

My father the bookseller used to tell me, "Every movement needs materials. Even God wrote a book." I like that. Of all the methods God could have chosen to talk about his movement to restore us to right relationship with him, he chose to write a book. So how did God, who is Spirit, put his words into a format that we could read and understand? He did it by *inspiration*. To inspire means "to breathe or blow into." Using the Holy Spirit, God literally breathed his words into 40 different writers (called "prophets") over a 1,600-year time period so they could write down his message for humankind.

> All Scripture is inspired by God and is useful to teach us what is true and to make us realize what is wrong in our lives (2 Timothy 3:16).

> Above all, you must realize that no prophecy in Scripture ever came from the prophet's own understanding, or from human initiative. No, those prophets were moved by the Holy Spirit, and they spoke from God (2 Peter 1:20-21).

Inspiration doesn't mean "dictation." The Holy Spirit guided the authors' thoughts and judgments but allowed them to express their own personalities and writing styles. Think of inspiration as a divine influence. Given the number of writers involved and the great span of time it took to write the 66 books that would eventually be recognized as inspired, it's nothing short of a miracle that there is such consistency in the message from Genesis to Revelation.

And now, nearly 2,000 years after the last book was written, we have the incredible privilege to read those words guided by the same Holy Spirit who inspired the Scriptures in the first place. This should fill us with awe and wonder. The same Holy Spirit who breathed into the Bible writers breathes out God's Word directly into our minds and hearts so we can comprehend "what is true" about God, the world, and ourselves. Simpson observes,

> The Holy Scriptures are the breath of God. Just as He breathed into man the breath of life, and man became a living soul, so He has breathed into the Word His own life, and it is the expression of His thought, His mind, and His heart. Just as you breathe upon the window-pane, and the vapor clouds it, so God has breathed upon the page, and lo, His very thought and heart are there, not as dead letters, but as the living message of His love.[1]

This is what I want when I read the Bible. I want God to breathe on me so my mind and heart will be opened to the truth he wants to teach me. "We will never truly know the truth until we are taught by [the Holy Spirit]," writes Torrey.[2]

This concept of supernatural instruction isn't taught in churches today, at least not in the ones I have attended. And it isn't just the writers from a hundred years ago who frame the Holy Spirit and the Holy Scriptures in this way. Jordan Standridge, a pastor of evangelism writing for *The Cripplegate* blog, offers this reminder:

> Since it is the Holy Spirit who leads us into truth (John 16:13), it is foolish and outright dangerous

to show up and hear God's Word, or read it in our devotions, without asking the Lord to illumine our hearts and change us to love Him more.[3]

IF YOU ASK, HE WILL ANSWER

I am learning to read the Bible differently from the way I did before. Like many well-intentioned Christians, I used to open to a chapter or passage in the Bible and start reading. Invariably, the words would speak to me, but only on a superficial level. I was coming to the Word out of duty or devotion rather than from a desire to have a personal connection with the author.

Now my practice is more like a child coming to their parent with a book in hand. "Daddy, would you read to me?" It's a feeling of inadequacy combined with expectancy. I know I can't get to the depths of a verse or passage on my own, but more and more I am asking God my Father to help me, because Jesus promised the Holy Spirit would guide me into all truth.

I have started a new habit, and that is to pray before I read. I talk directly to the Holy Spirit, asking for understanding, wisdom, and insight. I ask for his words to burrow into my soul and change my heart. I want him to be my teacher, for only he can teach in this way.

> When the Father sends the Advocate as my representative—that is, the Holy Spirit—he will teach you everything and will remind you of everything I have told you (John 14:26).

According to Jesus, the Holy Spirit both teaches and reminds us. These seem to be two different but complementary activities. First, as Torrey reminds us, the Holy Spirit teaches.

> The Spirit will guide the one whom He thus teaches "into all the truth." The whole sphere of God's truth is for each one of us, but the Holy Spirit will not guide us into all the truth in a single day, nor in a week, nor in a year, but step by step.[4]

I like the concept of learning step by step. It implies that there is no time limit for this relationship we have with the Holy Spirit. We aren't taking a semester class to earn a grade. This is a lifetime process that will utterly change us.

I have a picture on my desk of my grandfather John, likely taken when he was about 80 years old. This was the father of my first dad, the one who died young. I didn't know this grandfather very well, but the photo speaks to me. In the photo, he is sitting in a chair, holding a Bible. He was a farmer and house painter, but he is wearing a suit and tie in this portrait. His eyes are focused on the pages of the Bible.

The image inspires me. I am filled with gratitude and respect for this otherwise ordinary man who had an extraordinary relationship with the Holy Spirit as he read the Scriptures.

REMINDING YOU OF JESUS

There's another benefit to the believers who ask the Holy Spirit for help in understanding God's Word. Not only does he help us with the written Word, but he also helps us remember the teachings of the living Word, Jesus Christ. Knowing that his disciples would need some divine influence when they got into a tight spot, Jesus gave them some practical advice:

> When you are brought to trial in the synagogues and before rulers and authorities, don't worry about how to defend yourself or what to say, for the Holy Spirit will teach you at that time what needs to be said (Luke 12:11-12).

I haven't yet had to stand before rulers and authorities to explain why I am a Christian, but I have been in situations where I have had no idea what I would say next, and something came to mind at just the right time. Many years ago I was asked to lead a discussion on the Mel Gibson movie *The Passion of the Christ*. The graphic portrayal of the suffering of Jesus deeply affected a wealthy Christian friend of mine. He decided to invite his neighbors to his home for a discussion about the movie, which was sweeping the country at the time. He asked if I would be willing to moderate the evening and answer questions about the film.

When I arrived, his spacious living room was full. Rumor had it that a famous writer who lived down the street was coming, but he didn't show, much to my relief. Admittedly, I was nervous because I figured successful people would not be shy about asking tough questions. And they weren't.

One of the questions was pointed and direct, almost to the point of being sacrilegious. Others in the room were as surprised by the question as I was. I can still see the look of shock on my friend's wife's face as I stood there, wondering what I was going to say. I prayed in my head, asking for help. Instantly, a coherent response came to my mind. The words flowed effortlessly, and they actually made sense.

As I answered, I could see a change in the body language of the person who had asked the question. He softened and looked like he was actually hearing what I was saying. Then I glanced at my friend's wife, who had looked like she was going to throw up just moments before. Her expression had changed from one of abject panic to warmth.

At that moment, and in many ways since then, I could identify with Simpson's conclusion about the power of the Holy Spirit to stir us in the depths of our being so we can respond with words we didn't know were there.

> Not only does He teach us, but He quickens our intellect to remember and to learn. He is the Author and the Illuminator of the mind, and He is the Spirit of suggestion. He knows how to bring back forgotten truths in the moment of need. He knows how to suggest the promise in the time of depression. He knows how to say, "It is written," and put into our hand the sword of the Spirit, when the adversary's wiles are trying and perplexing us.[5]

This is what the Holy Spirit does—what he longs to do—in our lives, if we just ask him. "He is ready to do it even more frequently," says Torrey, "if we only expect it of Him and look to Him to do it."[6]

A SUPERNATURAL ACT

Words are my living and my livelihood, but I'm not unique. Every person depends on words to live, learn, and understand. Words are a gift from God, and I believe he has been the instigator of every literary advancement in the history of the world: from the creation of the first genuine alphabet in the eighth century BC, to the invention of the codex in the first century and the printing press in the first half of the fifteenth century, to the digital revolution we are enjoying in our own lifetimes. All these advancements in the way content is displayed, distributed, and digested were part of God's plan to publish his story of love and redemption for the human race.

The word *publish* simply means to "make public." Whether words are made public in print, in digital format, or through audio or video, they are being published. Moody understood the power of publishing and the role of the Holy Spirit in that process. In addition to founding the Bible institute that bears his name, he founded a publishing company in the late nineteenth century. Here's what he wrote about the Bible and publishing:

> The disciples of Jesus were all filled with the Spirit, and the Word was published; and when the Spirit of God comes down upon the church, and we are anointed, the Word will be published in the streets, in the lanes and in the alleys; there will not be a dark cellar nor a dark attic, nor a home where the Gospel will not be carried by some loving heart, if the Spirit comes upon God's people in demonstration and in power.[7]

"Though words are not the only thing God specializes in," Wright observes, "they are a central part of his repertoire." Because God has chosen to communicate to us through his words, we need to see them for what they are and what they do for us. "Scripture...is one of the points where heaven and earth overlap and interlock."[8]

This is a thought almost too lofty for words. Whenever we read and study and meditate on the Word of God in the presence and power of the Holy Spirit, we are ushered into the throne room of God, where Jesus sits at God's right hand. Knowing this reality, the way we read and interact with Scripture should rise from the level of the mundane to the realm of the majestic. John Piper says it well:

> God intends for us to read his word in a way that involves actions and experiences of the human soul that are beyond ordinary human experience. *Seeing* the glory of Jesus is not merely with our ordinary physical eyes, but with "the eyes of [our] hearts" (Eph. 1:18).[9]

When we encounter Scripture through the Holy Spirit (or perhaps I should say, when the Scriptures encounter us), the curtain between earth and heaven is opened. There we stand with our hearts laid bare in the very presence of the Trinity for the express purpose of reflecting the glory of Jesus.

> All of us who have had that veil removed can see and reflect the glory of the Lord. And the Lord—who is the Spirit—makes us more and more like him as we are changed into his glorious image (2 Corinthians 3:18).

Oh, that our hearts would be illuminated as we read God's Word so we can comprehend the height and depth and width of Christ's love for us and the glory he deserves! Piper concludes,

> If we are going to succeed in reading, as God intends for us to read, it will have to be a supernatural act. God will have to take out the heart of stone, with its hardness and resistance to his glory, and put in a heart of flesh, with its living sensitivity to God's worth and beauty (Ezek. 11:19; 36:26).[10]

TWO EXTREMES TO AVOID

For most of my life I have been focused on the Bible to the exclusion of the Holy Spirit. There are many people like me. But there are also plenty of Christians who are focused on the Holy Spirit to the exclusion of the Bible.

Paul Miller, whose wonderful book *A Praying Life* has opened my eyes and heart to the power of prayer, calls these two groups "Word Only" and "Spirit Only" people.

Word Only people believe God speaks only through the Word. Spirit Only people believe that God speaks through the Spirit to the extent that his perceived voice has as much authority as the Word.

Word Only people focus strictly on the will of God and obedience to the Bible. Spirit Only people believe faith puts God into action on our behalf. (Essentially, God does what we want.)

Word Only people have more of a tendency toward legalism, proudly avoiding certain sins while failing to show love and mercy to others. Spirit Only people follow their feelings, believing God is speaking to them through their thoughts and impressions, which leaves the door open to selfish desires.

Word Only people adopt a kind of rationalistic view, where truth can be found through reason and logic. Spirit Only people believe truth can be found through their feelings and intuition.

The result of each of these routes is not good. Word Only people miss the "real time" communion with the Holy Spirit, while Spirit Only people are at the mercy of their feelings.[11]

In his book *Open to the Spirit,* Scot McKnight advises that we avoid these two extremes: diminishing the Spirit in our focus on the Bible, or diminishing the Bible in our focus on the Spirit. "We must not idolize the Bible to the exclusion of hearing from the Spirit," he writes.[12] Neither should we focus on the Spirit to the exclusion of learning from the Bible.

LIVE A BALANCED LIFE

There's no good reason why the Word and the Spirit cannot exist in equal measure in our lives. Miller writes,

> We need the sharp-edged, absolute character of the Word and the intuitive, personal leading of the Spirit. The Word provides the structure, the vocabulary. The Spirit personalizes it to our life. Keeping the Word and the Spirit together guards us from the danger of God-talk becoming a cover for our own desires and the danger of lives isolated from God.[13]

The Holy Spirit breathed in the Word we read, and he

breathes out through us as we read it. "The Spirit grabs us where we are and takes us into the presence of God," writes McKnight. "Then we are dropped back into our world, having experienced a fresh encounter with God."[14]

God's Word is more than words, more than a mere guidebook. Yes, it offers inspired information, instruction, and insight. But it also presents the Spirit-filled fuel we need to be the people God wants us to be, people who are "conformed to the image of his Son" (Romans 8:29 NIV). And yet, the Bible is no less than a guidebook for life, as long as we ask the Holy Spirit to help us fulfill this instruction given by the apostle Paul to the Colossian church:

> Let the word of Christ dwell in you richly, teaching and admonishing one another in all wisdom, singing psalms and hymns and spiritual songs, with thankfulness in your hearts to God (Colossians 3:16 ESV).

EVERYTHING YOU NEED

The most often-quoted Scripture verse about the benefits and sufficiency of God's Word comes from the pen of the apostle Paul, giving advice to a young pastor by the name of Timothy:

> All Scripture is inspired by God and is useful to teach us what is true and to make us realize what is wrong in our lives. It corrects us when we are wrong and teaches us to do what is right. God uses it to prepare and equip his people to do every good work (2 Timothy 3:16-17).

In *Bruce and Stan's Pocket Guide to Studying Your Bible*, a little book I wrote with Bruce Bickel, we looked at the promises contained in these two verses:

- **Motivation: *All Scripture is inspired by God...*** This should be all the reason we need to read the Word of God and follow what it says.

- **Instruction: *...and is useful to teach us what is true...*** We can trust the Bible to be true in everything it says.

- **Detection: *...and to make us realize what is wrong in our lives.*** Because the Bible is written by God, we can count on it to show us what we are doing wrong.

- **Correction: *It corrects us when we are wrong...*** After we find out what's wrong, the Bible will tell us how to fix the broken places with the power and presence of the Holy Spirit.

- **Direction: *...and teaches us to do what is right.*** We can't rely on our own impressions and instincts as a measurement for our lives. Because the Bible is God's book, we can count on it to give us a new and improved value system.

- **Preparation: *God uses it to prepare and equip his people...*** God's preparation comes through his Word and through his Spirit, who equips us in every way to do God's will and work.

- **Action:** *...to do every good work.* The Bible contains and the Spirit confirms everything we need to become—and to do—all that God has planned for us.[15]

A FEW GOOD HEARTS

In addition to the books by Murray, Moody, Simpson, Torrey, and Tozer that I found in my father's box, I also unearthed a Bible—my father's Bible. It was worn and underlined to some degree. Nothing excessive. But I could tell which verses were especially meaningful to him.

One verse in particular stood out because it was underlined in red, much like he had done in the books I had leafed through. As much as I could tell, it was my father's "life verse." Here it is:

> The eyes of the LORD search the whole earth in order to strengthen those whose hearts are fully committed to him (2 Chronicles 16:9).

If you've noticed one recurring theme in this chapter about the illumination of the Holy Spirit, I hope you have observed how often the heart comes into play. If I could sit down with my father today, I am convinced he would tell me his longing was to be the kind of person God would notice and strengthen because his heart was fully committed to the Father, Son, and Holy Spirit. That's what I want to do. That's who I want to be.

> I keep asking that the God of our Lord Jesus Christ, the glorious Father, may give you the Spirit of wisdom and revelation, so that you may

know him better. I pray that the eyes of your heart may be enlightened in order that you may know the hope to which he has called you, the riches of his glorious inheritance in his holy people, and his incomparably great power for us who believe (Ephesians 1:17-19 NIV).

CHAPTER 5

The Gifts of the Holy Spirit

I have a confession to make. For most of my Christian life I have operated as if my existence here on earth were the only thing that counts. Even though I believe in a supernatural God and have accepted his gift of salvation, made possible by his supernatural Son, I have not taken the supernatural world seriously.

Don't get me wrong. I have always believed in the supernatural (at least since that night in the backseat of my mother's car). But I have lived as if there were nothing more to this life than what I can see, hear, taste, and smell.

Maybe it's the effect of growing up in the Western world, heavily influenced by rational and scientific thought. Or perhaps it's because the churches I have attended throughout my life have been strong on the practical side of living as a Christian—love God, love your neighbor, read your Bible, give to missions, those sorts of things. All good and vital components of the Christian life.

But where has been my awe of the supernatural dimension of my faith? When have I read about miracles in the Bible and truly believed they could happen today? Oh, I believe I will go to a supernatural place when I die (or when Jesus returns), but that's for later. So far on earth, my life has been lived in the natural and ordinary rather than the supernatural and extraordinary.

In my journey to better know the Holy Spirit and his role in my life, I have come to understand that living on earth is anything but natural and ordinary. I am a temple of the Holy Spirit, both as an individual and as a member of the body of Christ. The third Person of the Trinity has regenerated me, indwelled me, and now fills me as I make room in my spiritual house. I have everything I need to live a supernatural life.

The thing is, every person on earth is a supernatural being based on these two facts: Every person has been created in God's image, and every one of us, regardless of belief, will live forever. C.S. Lewis put it this way:

> There are no *ordinary* people. You have never talked to a mere mortal. Nations, cultures, arts, civilisations—these are mortal, and their life is to ours as the life of a gnat. But it is immortals whom we joke with, work with, marry, snub, and exploit—immortal horrors or everlasting splendours.[1]

If we are truly supernatural beings, we need to live that way. And how do we do that? By acknowledging, discovering, and understanding how to use our supernatural power. To be clear, even though all people are immortal, not every person has supernatural power. Only those believers who are indwelled by the Holy Spirit have such power, which the Scriptures refer to as a spiritual gift.

YOU HAVE RECEIVED POWER

Until now, we have been talking mostly about the wind or breath of the Holy Spirit. In this chapter and the next we will be shifting to the fire of the Holy Spirit, which represents the power of God in our lives. This power is no metaphor for something less. This power is real, and there is more than you ever thought.

At the same upper room gathering where Jesus revealed to his disciples that the Holy Spirit—the Counselor, Helper, and Advocate—would be coming to them, he explained that they would have the ability to do "even greater works" than he did. Sometimes we read these words and think they are for those disciples in the room and not for us. But I want you to read these words of Christ as if they are for you—because they are!

> I tell you the truth, anyone who believes in me will do the same works I have done, and even greater works, because I am going to be with the Father. You can ask for anything in my name, and I will do it, so that the Son can bring glory to the Father. Yes, ask me for anything in my name, and I will do it! (John 14:12-14).

Is it possible we can do "even greater works" than Jesus did? Honestly, I never believed that. I thought that promise applied only to those first-century disciples. They watched Jesus heal the sick and raise the dead. The disciples were witnesses to the miracles of Jesus turning water into wine and feeding 5,000 people with a basketful of bread and fish. When Jesus told them they would do greater works than those, I figured such miracles were restricted to that time in history and had little to do with believers living today.

It turns out these "even greater works" have everything to do with you and me. But how is this possible?

Just before Jesus ascended into heaven, he explained to his disciples *how* this would be possible, reminding them of what he had told them in the upper room:

> Do not leave Jerusalem until the Father sends you the gift he promised, as I told you before. John baptized with water, but in just a few days you will be baptized with the Holy Spirit... You will receive power when the Holy Spirit comes upon you. And you will be my witnesses, telling people about me everywhere—in Jerusalem, throughout Judea, in Samaria, and to the ends of the earth (Acts 1:4-5,8).

This power is not just for those believers who watched Jesus ascend into heaven. This power is not just for a few Christians. This Holy Spirit power is for *all* those who have put their faith in Jesus Christ alone by faith alone. This power is for you and for me. And here's a little secret: You don't even have to ask for it. You already have the supernatural power Jesus promised. Your power is your spiritual gift or gifts, given to you by the Holy Spirit.

"A spiritual gift is any ability that is empowered by the Holy

Spirit and used in any ministry of the church," writes Wayne Grudem.[2] This is absolutely key. Spiritual gifts are dispensed by the Holy Spirit to each Christian for the purpose of building up the body of Christ. As we dig into just what these gifts are all about, we will discover that every one of them—from serving to healing—is a supernatural power given to us by the Holy Spirit.

HOW SPIRITUAL GIFTS WORK

There are several passages in the Bible that give us specific instructions on spiritual gifts and how they work. To get us going, here is a passage from one of the letters the apostle Paul wrote to the church at Corinth. Turns out the Corinthians were a lot like us, even though we are separated from them by 2,000 years.

> Now, dear brothers and sisters, regarding your question about the special abilities the Spirit gives us. I don't want you to misunderstand this. You know that when you were still pagans, you were led astray and swept along in worshiping speechless idols. So I want you to know that no one speaking by the Spirit of God will curse Jesus, and no one can say Jesus is Lord, except by the Holy Spirit.
>
> There are different kinds of spiritual gifts, but the same Spirit is the source of them all. There are different kinds of service, but we serve the same Lord. God works in different ways, but it is the same God who does the work in all of us.
>
> A spiritual gift is given to each of us so we can help each other (1 Corinthians 12:1-7).

From this passage and others, we can know at least three things about how spiritual gifts actually work. First, the Holy Spirit chooses the gift or gifts each of us has.

> It is the one and only Spirit who distributes all these gifts. He alone decides which gift each person should have (1 Corinthians 12:11).

Second, each of us has at least one gift.

> God has given each of you a gift from his great variety of spiritual gifts (1 Peter 4:10).

The key word here is *variety*. Or, to use a word that carries great meaning in our world, the Holy Spirit has designed and distributed a *diversity* of gifts. Just as the human body has many parts, all of which function together to make up a healthy body, so the body of Christ has a diversity of gifts. When they function together in a local church, great things happen.

Third, every spiritual gift is intended for the benefit of the Christian community known as the church. The Holy Spirit hasn't given you a spiritual gift for your own personal enjoyment. Instead, you are to use it to help others.

> A spiritual gift is given to each of us so we can help each other (1 Corinthians 12:7).

WHY THE CHURCH?

The presence of spiritual gifts in our lives is as good a reason as any for staying connected to a local church. It's become fashionable in recent years for people to abandon the church in favor of a more "authentic" spiritual experience. There's no question some people have been harmed—emotionally, psychologically, spiritually, and sometimes physically—in a church. Damage in any form is inexcusable and should be reported if not remedied.

But leaving a church because it doesn't measure up to some kind of unrealistic or unattainable standard is counterproductive for one simple reason. When you aren't connected to a body of believers who worship together, hear sound biblical teaching, and participate in baptism and communion, you are disconnected from the spiritual gifts that others can offer you and that you can offer others.

To use Paul's organic "body of Christ" analogy, leaving a church to go it alone would be like the head saying to the feet, "I don't need you" (1 Corinthians 12:21). In fact, we do need one another, and this matter of spiritual gifts is the primary reason why. As Tozer observes,

> It is in the setting of the local church that the Holy Spirit does his best work. Nowhere else can the Holy Spirit be seen better. That is why the Spirit-filled church is so crucial in our day and age. The church started in apostolic times with Spirit-filled congregations and nothing has changed to disqualify that.[3]

FOUR CHARACTERISTICS OF THE SPIRIT-FILLED CHURCH

Just as we are commanded to be filled with the Holy Spirit so his truth, goodness, and beauty can shine in our lives, a

Spirit-filled church will reflect the power and wonders of the Holy Spirit. Tozer reflects on this idea of the church being "Spirit filled."

> I believe a Spirit-filled church will reflect the beauty and harmony of the Holy Spirit. It will be an unlimited beauty, growing year by year and generation by generation. It is in the Spirit-filled church that the Holy Spirit delights to reveal Himself and do the work He is longing to do.[4]

Tozer lists four characteristics of the Spirit-filled church that were true when the church was born after Jesus ascended into heaven and are just as true today.

Unity

The reason the body of Christ functions together is because we have been baptized by one Spirit (1 Corinthians 12:13). Simpson observes,

> The church is not an organization. It is an organic life; it is a living body constituted by the Holy Ghost, and united to Jesus Christ, its life and living Head.[5]

The Spirit-filled church shows the "supreme unity" of the people who come together to worship and use their gifts in the service of others, so that Jesus may be glorified. "We come together because there is one thing we focus on, and that is the Lord Jesus Christ."[6]

Authority

"The Spirit-filled church recognizes and honors the authority of the Holy Spirit," writes Tozer. Essentially this means that the church is sensitive to and seeks the leading of the Holy Spirit through the hearts and minds of those who regularly gather together. Tozer makes a striking suggestion:

> What is needed today is for churches to call a moratorium on all activity for six months, get together on our knees, and wait upon the Holy Spirit to move in the direction He wants us to go.[7]

Exaltation of Christ

This characteristic goes back to the "one big thing" the Holy Spirit does in the life of the believer. It applies just as strongly to his work in the church. The most basic work of the Holy Spirit in the life of any person and any church is to "lift up" Jesus Christ. "When I am lifted up on the cross," Jesus said, "I will draw everyone to me" (John 12:32 TLB).

One of the things I look for in any sermon or Bible study is the way the preacher or teacher points to Jesus. If Jesus is missing, I am disappointed. I know this oversight is not intentional, but it means something else besides Jesus is being exalted.

> Of course, we use the name of Jesus in our prayers, hoping that will get us somewhere in our praying. We would say nothing negative about Jesus Christ. However, when we come to church, instead of exalting Jesus Christ, we exalt personalities,

celebrities, and programs. Often this is what brings us together, which is a pseudo-unity that will never endure.[8]

Harmony of the Gifts

Because the Holy Spirit dispenses and directs the spiritual gifts, you can count on him to make sure that any local church, no matter the size, will have a harmony and unity of gifts. One gift won't dominate, nor will there be any gifts that are lacking. Furthermore, the gifts aren't necessarily related to positions in the church. For example, you don't have to be the pastor of your church to have the gift of teaching. And the pastor may have a gift other than teaching.

The basic principle here is that the gifts of the Spirit "are never at the discretion of any person, and they are definitely not religious toys to entertain us."[9] The gifts are under the direction of the Holy Spirit, and it's up to him to feature any one gift at a particular time.

When it comes to the gifts of the Spirit, we can have confidence that there will be harmony and unity because all three members of the Trinity are involved. Notice how the Holy Spirit, Jesus, and the Father are all involved in giving and using spiritual gifts:

> There are different kinds of spiritual gifts, but the same Spirit is the source of them all. There are different kinds of service, but we serve the same Lord. God works in different ways, but it is the same God who does the work in all of us (1 Corinthians 12:4-6).

THE SPIRITUAL GIFTS

Most of the teaching in the Bible about spiritual gifts comes from the apostle Paul, with a brief mention from Peter. Here are the spiritual gifts listed from four different passages:

Romans 12:6-8

God has given us different gifts for doing certain things well (verse 6).

Prophecy	Encouragement	Kindness
Serving	Giving	
Teaching	Leadership	

1 Corinthians 12:4-11

There are different kinds of spiritual gifts (verse 4).

Wisdom	Healing	Discernment
Knowledge	Miracles	Tongues
Faith	Prophecy	Interpretation

Ephesians 4:11

These are the gifts Christ gave to the church.

Apostle	Evangelist	Teacher
Prophet	Pastor	

1 Peter 4:10-11

God has given each of you a gift from his great variety of spiritual gifts. Use them well to serve one another (verse 10).

Speaking	Service

FIVE KINDS OF GIFTS

Bruce Bickel and I wrote a little book called *Bruce and Stan's Pocket Guide to Knowing the Holy Spirit*, and in it we classify the 18 gifts listed in the Bible passages I just referenced. (There are actually 23 gifts listed in these passages, but as you noticed, there are some duplications.) Following is a summary of those categories.[10]

Discerning Gifts: The Power to Know

Knowledge—One view of this spiritual gift is to see it as the supernatural ability to have knowledge of something that would be impossible to know except by divine revelation. This is a bit tricky because there may be no way to verify if the person giving a word of knowledge is speaking from their own gut or from a true, God-given revelation. A more "conservative" approach is to see this gift as the result of accumulated wisdom enhanced by the Holy Spirit for a particular situation. Because I have seen the use of this gift firsthand, I believe there are those who are given special insights by the Holy Spirit for a particular situation based on no prior knowledge.

Wisdom—This gift may be more common, at least in my experience. Many times I have been puzzled by a particular problem, and I sought the advice of someone I knew to be wise. Invariably, they offered a perspective or solution that went beyond mere human understanding. You know when wisdom is from God because it is so profound and so spot on. I believe my father the bookseller had the spiritual gift of wisdom. He had unusual insight and without fail would give me an answer to a problem that I would not have considered on my own.

Discernment—This gift is related to wisdom, but it applies more to the discernment of truth. Oftentimes there are situations where two viewpoints seem very close, especially when it comes to interpreting Scripture. Someone with the gift of discernment will come up with the best viewpoint, and often they will be able to distinguish truth from error. People with this gift protect the Christian community from accepting false teaching. Having said that, it's imperative for all maturing Christians to learn the truth of God's Word through study and prayer.

Dynamic Gifts: The Power to Do

Faith—Every Christian is saved by faith alone in Christ alone, but there is a spiritual gift of faith that enables someone to have a supernatural confidence (the word *confidence* literally means "with faith") in God's ability to provide, protect, and deliver on his promises. Sometimes people with this gift will be criticized for being overly trusting—that is, until the very thing they hoped for actually happens.

Miracles—This gift and the one that follows are controversial in that Christians disagree over how they apply today. There are some, called *cessationists*, who believe the so-called "spectacular" gifts of miracles, healing, and prophecy were for the apostolic age, when these gifts were necessary signs of the supernatural power of God in the natural world. But cessationists believe that at some point the Holy Spirit stopped or "ceased" dispensing these gifts. I don't agree with this viewpoint because it is inconsistent with the pattern of Christ's teaching, not to mention the evidence in our world today that miracles still occur.

Writing more than a hundred years ago, A.J. Gordon, founder of the school that eventually became Gordon College, responded this way concerning the continuation of the gifts of miracles and healing:

> Whatever practical difficulties we may have in regard to the fulfillment of this word, these ought not to lead us to limit it where the Lord has not limited it... The only safe position is to assert emphatically the perpetuity of the promise, and with the same emphasis to admit the general weakness and failure of the Church's faith in appropriating it... We conclude, therefore, that... the miraculous gifts were bestowed to abide *in the Church* to the end, though not that every believer should be endowed with them.[11]

In fact, every writer I found in my father's box of books—Murray, Moody, Simpson, Torrey, and Tozer—believed the gifts of miracles and healing to be in full force today. Not surprisingly, to the moment of his death, my father believed in the gift of healing.

Healing—Perhaps no spiritual gift comes with more controversy than this one. I believe our skepticism about healing is informed by the charlatans and false teachers who have appropriated this gift for their own glory and enrichment. Sadly, many of these false healers have a large public platform and therefore contribute to the contempt of the larger culture toward the whole of Christianity.

Perhaps more serious is the damage these wolves in sheep's clothing have done to Christians. We have been so discouraged by the counterfeit healers out there that we fail to believe that God still heals. Furthermore, because we have a tendency to emphasize the gift of *physical* healing, we overlook the fact that God's healing is for every dimension of our lives.

I attend a Presbyterian church, a denomination not exactly known for promoting the gift of healing. But during the season of Lent, as I am writing this chapter, I received an announcement that our church is holding a service for healing. Here's the description for this special time:

> At this service, we will focus on that aspect of God's character, bringing to God our own frailty and brokenness—felt not just in physical illness, but also in guilt, anxiety and all the burdens that weigh us down. Above all, we will come to God, who knows our needs before we ask and whose love is stronger than suffering and even death.

As I said, my father believed in healing until his dying breath. That may seem incongruous, and I will admit that his belief in healing and the actual outcome of his physical life here on earth have been a source of puzzlement for me. I have come to believe that my father was indeed healed, though not physically. I believe he experienced the peace and love of God through his suffering and death. He may not have been healed physically, but he was healed spiritually, which is the far greater miracle. After all, our lives here on earth are "like the morning fog"—here for a while and then gone (James 4:14). By comparison, our lives in Christ are eternal, as we will spend our endless days in the presence of our beautiful Savior.

At the same time, God does still heal physically. I have

seen it in the lives of friends and strangers, and so have you. Simpson had this to say about this spiritual gift in regard to his own healing. Notice how he phrased his words in the form of a promise:

> I solemnly accept this truth as part of Thy Word…
> I take the Lord Jesus as my physical life… I sol-
> emnly agree to use this blessing for the glory of
> God, and the good of others, and to speak of it
> or minister in connection with it in any way in
> which God may call me or others may need me
> in the future.[12]

Declaring Gifts: The Power to Say

Prophecy—This gift is not as tricky as it seems because you know for sure if a prophetic utterance is true simply by the outcome. As I write this, a popular Bible teacher in a local church has predicted that a massive earthquake and tsunami will strike California. Now that in itself isn't much of a proph-ecy since scientists have been predicting such a catastrophic event for some time (and yet I continue to live in Southern California—go figure!). The difference is that this teacher, who claims to have the gift of prophecy, has set a particular date for the earthquake and tsunami to occur.

If by the time you are reading this the California coast has indeed fallen into the sea, then you may want to find out who this prophet is and hear what else they are predicting. But if the prophecy turns out to be a dud, then there's only one con-clusion you can reach: This was a false prophecy given by a false prophet. And if you need more proof, the reactions of

God and Jesus to false prophets should convince you to steer clear of such people.

> Because what you say is false and your visions are a lie, I will stand against you, says the Sovereign Lord (Ezekiel 13:8).

> Beware of false prophets who come disguised as harmless sheep but are really vicious wolves (Matthew 7:15).

Just like we tend to overemphasize the physical aspect of healing, we put too much stock in the kind of prophecy known as *foretelling*, when we should pay more attention to prophecy known as *forthtelling*. Even in the Old Testament times, the prophets of God spent most of their time relaying God's message of repentance and hope to his people. Revealing God's future plans was not the biggest part of their jobs as prophets.

In the same way, the gift of prophecy today will more often refer to a specific message God wants delivered to his people. In these cases, those with the gift of prophecy would be characterized as having a "prophetic voice."

Tongues—Here's another spiritual gift subject to abuse, which is a shame. The gift of tongues isn't babbling incoherently. This is the supernatural gift of being able to speak in a language that is not known to the person who is speaking it. The day of Pentecost, which occurred seven weeks after Jesus' resurrection, is the best example of the demonstration of this gift. This was when the Holy Spirit came upon the roughly 120 believers who had gathered together in Jerusalem. Here's the account from the book of Acts (notice the presence of wind and fire):

> Suddenly, there was a sound from heaven like the roaring of a mighty windstorm, and it filled the house where they were sitting. Then, what looked like flames or tongues of fire appeared and settled on each of them. And everyone present was filled with the Holy Spirit and began speaking in other languages, as the Holy Spirit gave them this ability (Acts 2:2-4).

People from many nations were gathered in Jerusalem for Pentecost, and each heard the believers speak in their language (verses 5-11). This was the spiritual gift of tongues in its purest form.

Many years ago I attended a conference of Spanish publishers. The speaker at one of the plenary events was a Caucasian like me, but this guy could speak perfect Spanish. I thought his ability was the result of years of language study. Turns out he received the gift of Spanish from a pastor who laid hands on him and prayed for him to receive the gift of being able not only to speak, but also to read and write Spanish—instantly. That, my friend, is the gift of tongues at its best.

Interpretation—This gift is the ability to interpret a message being spoken in tongues so that the group can understand what is being said. In this case, the language doesn't necessarily have to be a known language, such as Spanish. But if it's a spiritual language, it will fall on deaf ears unless someone with the gift of interpretation is present to convey the meaning. Paul was very clear that no one was to speak in tongues unless the message could be interpreted (see 1 Corinthians 14:27-28).

Discipling Gifts: The Power to Instruct

Apostleship—The title of *apostle* suggests "one who is sent." Originally, this referred to the disciples who knew and followed Jesus personally while he was on earth and then established churches after Pentecost. (Paul was called an apostle because Jesus encountered him on the road to Damascus.) The gift of apostleship today is found in those who are establishing churches around the world, just as the early apostles did.

Pastoring—This spiritual gift is the ability to "shepherd" the people in a local church. It's not just preaching or teaching (although a pastor could have those spiritual gifts as well), but leading, caring for, and protecting the people in his or her "flock."

Teaching—There are many teachers of the Word of God, and most aren't pastors. They teach Bible studies, classes, and small groups, with students ranging from children to adults. Those who have the gift of teaching have a supernatural ability to explain the truth of God's Word in a way that is correct as well as practical and relevant. When you hear the Bible explained from people with the gift of teaching, you know they have the gift because the Holy Spirit will confirm it in your own heart.

Encouragement—Another word for this spiritual gift is *exhortation*. People with this supernatural ability encourage people in their spiritual lives, bringing strength, confidence, and sometimes healing to others who are discouraged.

Evangelism—This spiritual gift refers to proclaiming the gospel message to people who haven't heard it before. There are many examples of evangelists throughout history who brought the good news of Christ to people outside the church. Moody and Torrey were both evangelists, and they traveled the world preaching the gospel with exceptional clarity in a way that invited the Holy Spirit to truly convict people of their need for Christ. However, most people who have the gift of evangelism don't preach to big crowds. They simply talk to people one on one, but with a fervor and conviction that stirs the hearts and souls of those who listen, pointing them to the one true Savior, Jesus Christ.

Disposition Gifts: The Power to Serve

Giving—This gift is not tied to the amount of money someone gives. True, people with the gift of giving can give large amounts of money, but this spiritual gift has more to do with sacrifice and unusual generosity, like the kind shown by the widow who was commended by Jesus for giving all she had (Mark 12:41-44). It was said of Kenneth Taylor, the founder of Tyndale House Publishers, that he never had a dollar he didn't want to give away. In fact, the Tyndale House Foundation, established early in his publishing career, has given hundreds of millions of dollars to missions and the work of Bible translation.

Kindness (mercy)—Every one of us should be aware of and sensitive to the needs of others so we can comfort them. But most of us miss a lot of opportunities simply because we are oblivious to the need. Those with the gift of mercy know when to act and what to do on behalf of those in need.

Serving—This gift can take many forms, and of course all

of us should constantly be looking for ways to serve others. But those with the spiritual gift of serving are empowered by the Holy Spirit to step into action and get the job done when the rest of us overlook the need.

Leadership (administration)—Not everyone in leadership has the gift of administration, which isn't a bad thing. Sometimes leaders need people to put their plans and vision into practice. Those with this gift have exceptional judgment and possess the skill set to organize and implement plans proposed by others.

HOW TO DISCOVER YOUR SPIRITUAL GIFT

The Bible isn't direct about ways to discover our spiritual gifts, so we need to use our heads and our hearts when it comes to identifying what gift or gifts we have and how we can use them. My advice is that you start at the source. Since the Holy Spirit is the one who gave you your gift, ask him to reveal it to you. You may not hear a voice, but you will begin to get a sense for your gift or gifts, especially as you take the next steps in the process of discovery.

Since spiritual gifts are distributed to build up the body of Christ, the next stop on your journey of discovery should be your church. Ask your pastor where there is a need. If you're shy about this and concerned that your pastor won't have time to help you, think again. The sweetest words a pastor can hear are "Is there a place in the church where I could serve?"

Get involved in some of the ministries in your church so you can begin to recognize in yourself a special sensitivity and desire in a certain area. Be careful about confusing your natural ability with your spiritual gift. A natural ability is likely due to genetics and is with you from birth. But your spiritual gift is given to you at the time you respond to the conviction of the Holy Spirit and become a Christian.

As you begin to use your spiritual gift, other people will see God at work in your life in ways you didn't anticipate. Most of all, when you are using your supernatural gift, you will have a sense of God's presence and power in your life as you realize that things are happening you could not or would not do on your own.

Spiritual gifts should produce a sense of deep humility rather than pride because you know they are coming from the Holy Spirit, not from your own ability.

LOVE ABOVE ALL

Paul concludes his discourse on spiritual gifts in 1 Corinthians 12 with a statement that should get our attention. After advising us to desire "the most helpful gifts," he makes a disclaimer:

> Now let me show you a way of life that is best of all (1 Corinthians 12:31).

What follows in 1 Corinthians 13 is perhaps the most famous chapter in all of Scripture, a beautiful call for love to define our lives and actions above all else. No matter what spiritual gifts you have, they are as meaningless as a loud gong or clanging cymbal if you don't have love.

As we conclude this chapter, take a moment to settle yourself, open your Bible and read this powerful and moving essay on love, inspired by the Holy Spirit. Ask the Spirit to speak to you through the words that have moved millions upon millions of people since they were first written.

> There are three things that remain—faith, hope, and love—and the greatest of these is love (1 Corinthians 13:13 TLB).

CHAPTER 6

The Power of the Holy Spirit

F ire and wind are two useful biblical pictures for the work of the Holy Spirit in our lives. *Fire* gives us an image of the Holy Spirit's *power*, and *wind* helps us think about the *presence* of the Holy Spirit. Both of these descriptive elements have popped up throughout the preceding chapters, but mostly we've been focused on the Holy Spirit's presence. In this chapter, we're turning our attention to his power in our lives.

We'll start by talking about water. I know, water and fire don't mix—but you will get the big picture as this chapter unfolds. You will see how, in a spiritual sense, water doesn't quench but actually leads to fire.

Earlier, I shared Ezekiel's dramatic vision of the valley of dry bones (Ezekiel 37:1-10). This prophetic narrative describes the miracle of giving life to those who are spiritually dead. It's a cinematic-style picture of the Holy Spirit's work in bringing dead souls to life.

Later in the book of Ezekiel, the prophet records another vision, this one less dramatic but no less important to us as regenerated children of God. The vision of the valley of dry bones shows us how God replaces our hearts of stone with hearts of flesh by the power of the Holy Spirit (Ezekiel 36:26). The vision we're about to see, that of water flowing from the temple, paints a picture of the living water given by Jesus through the Holy Spirit. Jesus may have had this prophecy in mind when he said in John 7:37-39,

> "Anyone who is thirsty may come to me! Anyone who believes in me may come and drink! For the Scriptures declare, 'Rivers of living water will flow from his heart.'" (When he said "living water," he was speaking of the Spirit, who would be given to everyone believing in him.)

As you read about this vision in Ezekiel 47, keep three things in mind:

1. This prophecy is for the nation of Israel, but the vision might equally be applied to the spiritual growth of Christians.

2. Jesus is the source of the water, and the river itself is a symbol of the Holy Spirit.

3. The river heals, revives, and helps produce fruit (verses 6-12).

WATER FLOWING FROM THE TEMPLE

In my vision, the man brought me back to the entrance of the Temple. There I saw a stream flowing east from beneath the door of the Temple and passing to the right of the altar on its south side. The man brought me outside the wall through the north gateway and led me around to the eastern entrance. There I could see the water flowing out through the south side of the east gateway.

Measuring as he went, he took me along the stream for 1,750 feet and then led me across. The water was up to my ankles. He measured off another 1,750 feet and led me across again. This time the water was up to my knees. After another 1,750 feet, it was up to my waist. Then he measured another 1,750 feet, and the river was too deep to walk across. It was deep enough to swim in, but too deep to walk through (Ezekiel 47:1-5).

I love this picture of the Christian experience. It shows the benefit of going deeper, a profitable practice in many areas of life, whether in relationships or reading or exploring the deep truths of God. "It is good to be often searching into the things of God, and trying the depth of them," writes Matthew Henry, "not only to look on the surface of those waters, but to go to the bottom of them as far as we can, to be often digging, often diving, into the mysteries of the kingdom of heaven, as those who covet to be intimately acquainted with those things."[1]

Ankle-Deep Water

When we respond to the Holy Spirit's conviction by acknowledging our sins and saying yes to the forgiveness of those sins through the death and resurrection of Jesus, we step into ankle-deep water. This is the place where spiritually regenerated lives begin. The Holy Spirit transforms and indwells us, and we feel the full assurance and safety of our faith in Christ. "If God is for us, who can be against us?" (Romans 8:31 NIV).

Knee-Deep Water

As we begin maturing in our Christian walk, we naturally step into knee-deep water. This is where we respond to the command to be filled with the Holy Spirit. Some commentators say the water to the knees represents prayer. I like that image. Prayer is a two-way spiritual street, whereby we confess our sins so the Holy Spirit can fill us. Prayer is how we hear the voice of the Holy Spirit. Knee-deep water is also where we get serious about reading and studying God's Word and doing what it says, relying on the illumination of the Holy Spirit for understanding and application. As a result, our lives begin to produce the fruit of the Spirit.

Waist-Deep Water

This is the next stage of spiritual maturity. As the King James Version of the Bible puts it, the water is up to our loins (Ezekiel 47:4). The loins represent strength, which speaks of spiritual power. This is where we discover and use our spiritual gift or gifts to serve the body of Christ. The effect of your life on others at this stage can be profound and fulfilling, but there is yet another level of spiritual depth.

Deep Enough to Swim In

This stage in the river represents the deepest spiritual level any believer can reach. When you are in the deep, you have gone beyond your own ability. You no longer support yourself, but rest in the power of the Holy Spirit. "This is what true spiritual maturity is all about," writes Alan Carr. "It is about coming to the end of ourselves and understanding that there is no way that we could ever do it on our own."[2] Commenting on the effect of Ezekiel's vision, Henry writes,

> If we search into the things of God, we shall find some things very plain and easy to be understood, as the waters that were but to the ankles, others more difficult, and which require a deeper search, as the water to the knees or the loins, and some quite beyond our reach… It is our wisdom, as the prophet here, to begin with that which is most easy…before we proceed to that which is dark and hard to be understood.[3]

DARK AND HARD TO UNDERSTAND

When Henry characterizes this wisdom as "dark," he doesn't mean sinister. This is the kind of dark that you experience in deep water. It's more difficult to see with our natural eyes and harder to understand. This is where we are going to discover the power of the Holy Spirit.

When most Christians reflect on the power of the Spirit, they tend to think in terms of "signs and wonders"—tongues, miracles, prophetic utterances, and the like. Maybe that's why the church tradition that shaped my view of the Holy Spirit rarely talked about his power, preferring to focus on the "practical" side of the Holy Spirit's work—regeneration, indwelling, baptizing, filling, and gifting.

As I have already said, I realize now how misguided I was and how much I was missing.

If you are part of the "signs and wonders" tradition, don't assume that the Holy Spirit's power is all that and nothing else. What I have discovered is that the sign gifts—tongues, miracles, and prophecy—are not necessarily the direct result of the Spirit's power. In fact, they have more of a connection to spiritual gifts and very little to do with the kind of power we're going to talk about.

My discovery of the Holy Spirit's work in the life of the believer has come primarily from books written long ago, many at the turn of the twentieth century, before the modern Pentecostal movement took off. This was certainly the case with most of the volumes I found in my father's box—with the exception of the works of Tozer, whose best-known books were written in the 1940s and '50s.

I tell you this because most of these authors expressed their views and experiences of the Holy Spirit before the birth of the modern Pentecostal movement during the Azusa Street Revival in 1906. Since that time, the average Christian has equated the Pentecostal and charismatic experience with signs and wonders. As a consequence, two opposite views of the Holy Spirit and his work in the life of the believer have emerged. One view (the one I grew up with) makes too little of the Holy Spirit, overemphasizing the Bible and relying too much on intellectual knowledge. The other makes too much of personal experiences with the Holy Spirit, underemphasizing Scripture and relying too much on felt knowledge.

THE BAPTISM OF THE HOLY SPIRIT— THE REST OF THE STORY

In chapter 2 we talked about the baptism of the Holy Spirit as the process by which the Spirit brings us into the body of Christ. "We have all been baptized into one body by one Spirit, and we all share the same Spirit" (1 Corinthians 12:13). This is the work of the Spirit to regenerate us, resulting in our salvation.

In the Pentecostal tradition there is another baptism of the Holy Spirit, usually referred to as the "second baptism" or "second blessing" of the Holy Spirit, and it's typically accompanied by signs and wonders.

Torrey and his contemporaries tell a different story. These deeply spiritual writers agree that this second baptism *with* the Spirit is distinct from the work of regeneration, but it is intended for service, not signs.

> In regeneration there is the impartation of life by the Spirit's power, and the one who receives it is saved; in baptism with the Holy Spirit, there is the impartation of power, and the one who receives it is fitted for service.[4]

Torrey draws upon the pronouncement of John the Baptist, who made a distinction between baptism with water, which results in regeneration, and baptism with the Holy Spirit, which results in power (notice the reference to fire).

> I baptize with water those who repent of their sins and turn to God. But someone is coming soon who is greater than I am—so much greater that I'm not worthy even to be his slave and carry his sandals. He will baptize you with the Holy Spirit and with fire (Matthew 3:11).

Jesus repeated this phrasing before he ascended into heaven.

> Once when he was eating with them, he commanded them, "Do not leave Jerusalem until the Father sends you the gift he promised, as I told you before. John baptized with water, but in just a few days you will be baptized with the Holy Spirit" (Acts 1:4-5).

FIRE AND WIND

The thing is, at this point the disciples were already Christians, and they had already received the Holy Spirit (John 20:22). So what John the Baptist prophesied and Jesus affirmed is that Jesus' followers would be baptized with the Holy Spirit a second time in a way that was distinct from the Holy Spirit's baptism with water (regeneration). That second time occurred on the day of Pentecost. Notice the presence of fire and wind in this dramatic scene.

> On the day of Pentecost, all the believers were meeting together in one place. Suddenly, there was a sound from heaven like the roaring of a mighty windstorm, and it filled the house where they were sitting. Then, what looked like flames

or tongues of fire appeared and settled on each of them. And everyone present was filled with the Holy Spirit and began speaking in other languages, as the Holy Spirit gave them this ability (Acts 2:1-4).

Because these early believers spoke in tongues, the Pentecostal tradition has picked up on this as the norm for those who have received the second baptism of the Holy Spirit. But in this well-known example, the believers spoke in the languages of the people who were in Jerusalem, who "were bewildered to hear their own languages being spoken by the believers" (Acts 2:6). The gift of tongues in known languages was for the purpose of *service*, to bring the saving message of Christ to lost people, not for personal edification.

Torrey's analysis in this regard is eerily prescient, even though these words were written in 1910:

> There are many Christians who in seeking the baptism with the Spirit are seeking personal ecstasy and rapture. They go to conventions and conferences for the deepening of the Christian life and come back and tell what a wonderful blessing they have received, referring to some new ecstasy that has come into their heart, but when you watch them, it is difficult to see that they are any more useful to their pastors or their churches than they were before, and one is compelled to think that whatever they have received, they have not received the real baptism with the Holy Spirit.
>
> Ecstasies and raptures are all right in their places. When they come, thank God for them...but in

a world such as we live in today, where sin and self-righteousness and unbelief are so triumphant, where there is such an awful tide of men, women, and young people sweeping on toward eternal perdition, I would rather go through my whole life and never have one touch of ecstasy but have power to witness for Christ and win others for Christ and thus save them than to have raptures 365 days in the year but no power to stem the awful tide of sin, to bring men, women, and children to a saving knowledge of my Lord and Savior Jesus Christ.[5]

THE POWER TO BE USEFUL

Martyn Lloyd-Jones, born in 1899, was a Welsh medical doctor and pastor who served as the minister of Westminster Chapel in London. His teaching on the "power and renewal" of the Holy Spirit makes a distinction between being filled with the Spirit and being baptized with the Spirit.

When we respond to the command in Ephesians 5:18 to "be filled with the Holy Spirit," the fruit of the Spirit will be evident in our lives. This is when the Holy Spirit can do his work of developing our character. That's why "the fruit of the Spirit... is a process," writes Lloyd-Jones. "This is the result of the indirect, constant, regular work of the Spirit within us as he uses the word and the teaching and example of others and fellowship with others—thus the fruit of the Spirit is produced in us."[6]

On the other hand:

> The first result of the baptism with the Spirit, therefore, is not the fruit of the Spirit, but experimental

evidence of the direct work of the Spirit upon us...
The primary purpose and function of the baptism
with the Spirit is beyond any question to enable
us to be witnesses to the Lord Jesus Christ and to
his great salvation.[7]

WILLING WITNESSES

Throughout Scripture there are examples of the triune
God seeking willing witnesses who will speak on behalf of his
plan to redeem fallen humanity. Sitting on his throne, with
the train of his robe filling the temple, the Lord cleansed and
called Isaiah to be a witness to the people of Israel.

> I heard the Lord asking, "Whom should I send as
> a messenger to this people? Who will go for us?" I
> said, "Here I am. Send me" (Isaiah 6:8).

In the New Testament, we read another dramatic story, this
one involving the apostle Paul prior to his conversion, when
he was known as Saul. From heaven, Jesus strikes Saul with
a blinding light and calls him to be a witness to the Gentiles.

> He fell to the ground and heard a voice saying to
> him, "Saul! Saul! Why are you persecuting me?"
>
> "Who are you, lord?" Saul asked.
>
> And the voice replied, "I am Jesus, the one you are
> persecuting! Now get up and go into the city, and
> you will be told what you must do" (Acts 9:4-6).

Fast-forward to the latter part of the nineteenth century in
America, where Moody was serving as a pastor and the leader

of a mission. People were coming to Christ under his ministry, but Moody wanted more. He wrote,

> I was crying all the time that God would fill me with His Spirit. Well, one day, in the city of New York—oh, what a day!—I cannot describe it, I seldom refer to it; it is almost too sacred an experience to name. Paul had an experience of which he never spoke for fourteen years. I can only say that God revealed Himself to me, and I had such an experience of His love that I had to ask Him to stay His hand.[8]

I could share similar accounts from Murray, Simpson, and Torrey—people baptized by the Holy Spirit for extraordinary service. There are those in our time, as well; men and women who have been infused with a sense of God's power and presence, who have become powerful witnesses to the Lord Jesus Christ and to his great salvation.

HOW DOES HE DO IT?

You may be wondering how the Holy Spirit goes about baptizing believers in this way. Here's how Murray explains it:

> Every tree grows from the root out of which it first sprang. The Day of Pentecost was the planting of the Christian church, and the Holy Spirit became the power of its life. Let us turn back to that experience and learn from the disciples what is really necessary. Attachment to Jesus, the abandonment of everything in the world for Him, despair of self

and of all help from man, holding on to the word
of promise, and then waiting on the living God—
this is the sure way of living in the joy and power
of the Holy Spirit.[9]

Lloyd-Jones warns that not all experiences are the exact
same. There is variation, as you saw in the three examples I
gave from the lives of Isaiah, Saul, and Moody. What these
experiences all have in common, however, is "first and fore-
most…a sense of the glory of God, an unusual sense of the
presence of God." Furthermore, the Holy Spirit makes real to
us the things we have previously believed.[10]

We talk about God and believe in God, but we don't *know*
God, at least not in the way we do when his power and presence—his fire and wind—come upon us to reveal his glory. As
Job said at the end of his long and emotional encounter with
God, "I had only heard about you before, but now I have seen
you with my own eyes. I take back everything I said, and I sit
in dust and ashes to show my repentance" (Job 42:5-6).

THE EXAMPLE
OF BILLY GRAHAM

In 2004 my wife and I attended Billy Graham's second-
to-last crusade, held at the Rose Bowl in Los Angeles. Shortly
before the crusade was held, Graham fell in his home and
injured his pelvis, requiring a stay in the hospital. He recov-
ered in time for the crusade and was able to preach on the
night we were there. The frail Graham, speaking from a wheel-
chair to a packed Rose Bowl crowd, described his recent injury
and hospitalization.

He was treated in a Catholic hospital, and on the wall in his room was an image of Christ on the cross. As Graham described it, he looked at the image and wept. Experiencing a deep sense of the presence of God, he was remorseful for his sin. He asked God for forgiveness and assurance that he was going to heaven. This was Billy Graham talking! My wife and I looked at each other—stunned, but also deeply moved.

Graham then began to give one of his patented invitations to receive Christ, but his words were muddled, his voice weak. It wasn't the typical call to salvation, but that didn't matter. Even before he could finish his call, people from every section of the Rose Bowl stood up and started making their way to the infield. As if reacting to what was taking place, the crusade choir quickly grabbed their song sheets and started singing "Just as I Am." Graham's voice trailed off, but it didn't matter. By virtue of the power and presence of the Holy Spirit, so evident and so real that evening, Graham's witness to the living Christ brought people out of their seats to the foot of the cross. It's a moment I will never forget.

There will be times when we feel less than certain about our faith. Our ability to articulate our beliefs may be muddled. Don't despair! If Billy Graham can experience times of doubt and weakness, so can we. Before the Holy Spirit baptized the Christians in Acts 2, they were uncertain and confused. But that uncertainty and confusion disappeared after the baptism of the Holy Spirit.

You can have power through the baptism of the Holy Spirit, a power that changes weaknesses into strengths. To quote Torrey, this baptism can change "cowards into heroes." To be clear, unlike the baptism *by* the Holy Spirit into the body of Christ, this baptism *with* the Holy Spirit is not a one-time experience.

As Torrey says, "We need a new filling for each new emergency of Christian service."[11]

EVIDENCE FOR THE BAPTISM

Besides the internal evidence of greater assurance and a sense of the manifest presence of God, there are some external evidences for baptism with the Holy Spirit. Lloyd-Jones cites Moses in the Old Testament and Stephen in the New Testament as two examples of people whose facial appearance reflected the glory of God.[12] "When Moses came down Mount Sinai carrying the two stone tablets inscribed with the terms of the covenant, he wasn't aware that his face had become radiant because he had spoken to the Lord" (Exodus 34:29). Similarly, when Stephen was falsely accused, arrested, and brought before the high priest, "everyone in the high council stared at Stephen, because his face became as bright as an angel's" (Acts 6:15).

When I was eight years old, in my first year with my mom and my new bookseller dad, I attended a child evangelism class in the home next door to ours. The leader of the class was a woman by the name of Emma Pop. She served as a teacher in that capacity for more than 30 years, and to this day I can see her face as she talked to us kids about Jesus. Hers wasn't just a kind and loving face, but a face that carried the sweetness of the Savior she loved so much. What I did not know is that her facial countenance was the reflection of the Holy Spirit's baptism and power in her life. I am convinced of that now.

The other evidence for the Holy Spirit's baptism is speech or preaching. Besides my story of Billy Graham's second-to-last crusade, many times in my life I have heard pastors and speakers who preached with anointed authority. In each case, the words were not conjured out of some carefully prepared speech. They were spoken from the heart and with great power. In one of his letters to the church at Corinth, Paul explains how this works.

> When I first came to you, dear brothers and sisters, I didn't use lofty words and impressive wisdom to tell you God's secret plan. For I decided that while I was with you I would forget everything except Jesus Christ, the one who was crucified. I came to you in weakness—timid and trembling. And my message and my preaching were very plain. Rather than using clever and persuasive speeches, I relied only on the power of the Holy Spirit. I did this so you would trust not in human wisdom but in the power of God (1 Corinthians 2:1-5).

A BAPTISM OF SERVICE, SACRIFICE, AND SUFFERING

There's a curious conversation recorded by Mark in his Gospel. Two of Jesus' disciples, the brothers James and John, ask Jesus for a favor. "When you sit on your glorious throne, we want to sit in places of honor next to you, one on your right and the other on your left" (Mark 10:37). Pretty bold. I guess that's why Jesus gave them the nickname "Sons of Thunder" (3:17).

Jesus answers them quickly and directly:

> You don't know what you are asking! Are you able to drink from the bitter cup of suffering I

am about to drink? Are you able to be baptized with the baptism of suffering I must be baptized with? (10:38).

The message is clear. This baptism is for service, for a great work God wants to do. It's the "baptism of suffering" experienced by Jesus. And then, to reinforce that sacrifice that will be required, Jesus tells them, "Whoever wants to be a leader among you must be your servant, and whoever wants to be first among you must be the slave of everyone else" (verses 43-44).

This is the essence of the baptism and power of the Holy Spirit we have been talking about in this chapter. It's a baptism of service, sacrifice, and suffering. Gordon writes,

> It costs much to obtain the power of the Spirit:
> it costs self-surrender and humiliation and the
> yielding up of our most precious things to God;
> it costs the perseverance of long waiting, and the
> faith of strong trust.[13]

Hudson Taylor (1832–1905), a medical doctor from London who is credited with opening China to the gospel, wrote openly about the consequences of what he called "the exchanged life" after he lost his wife and one-week-old child.

> When I think of my loss, my heart, nigh to breaking, rises in thankfulness to Him who has spared her such sorrow and made her so unspeakably happy. My tears are more tears of joy than grief. But most of all I joy in God through our Lord Jesus Christ—in His works, His ways, His providence, Himself.[14]

It is not my intention to inspire fear or to dissuade anyone from seeking this baptism of the Holy Spirit. But the perspective I am presenting should give us pause before we ask God for a special seat of honor next to Jesus. We need to "count the cost" (Luke 14:28) before seeking this power of the Holy Spirit.

DO YOU WANT THIS BAPTISM?

At the same time, if God is calling you to a special service beyond your natural abilities, something you could never do without the power of the Holy Spirit, Lloyd-Jones suggests four steps. I will summarize them here and go into more detail in the next chapter.

1. Recognize a need that is urgent—not a need you have, but a need of the church in the world.

2. Seek Jesus himself—to know him, love him, and be a witness for him. You may receive a wonderful experience, power, or special gifts, but the only way to receive these is to love Jesus.

3. Obey. This is crucial. God gives the Holy Spirit in power only to those who obey him. "You show the depth of your desire by the extent of your obedience."[15]

4. Pray for the blessing. Not just with an ordinary prayer, but with active, fervent, consistent, passionate prayers. "You plead the promises."[16] This was the path taken by Moody, Torrey,

Simpson, Gordon, and Hudson when they realized an urgent need.

> All these men had to pray, had to plead. They did not "take it by faith," or "demand" it, or "claim" it. Certainly not! They did all they could and yet they felt, "No we do not know, we have not felt this love; we want to know him." And then God in his own time answered them. The Lord baptized them with the Holy Spirit.[17]

Has God made you aware of a great need? Seek Jesus first, obey the voice of the Holy Spirit in your life, and plead with God in prayer. When your heart is right, God will find you and give you the strength you need through his Holy Spirit.

> The eyes of the LORD search the whole earth in order to strengthen those whose hearts are fully committed to him (2 Chronicles 16:9).

CHAPTER 7

The Holy Spirit, Your Advocate

Deep calls to deep
in the roar of your waterfalls;
all your waves and breakers
have swept over me.

PSALM 42:7 NIV

In our journey to unleash the power and presence of the Holy Spirit, we now find ourselves in deep water, too deep to find footing. We are in over our heads, at the mercy of the one who promises to hold us. We long to feel his power, but there are obstacles to overcome.

That's why we feel so unsettled and uncertain when we reach this place. This isn't just another step in the process of experiencing the power of the Holy Spirit. We are here because we have come to the end of ourselves. When we arrive in the deep, we expect to immediately find peace and calm. But first we will find ourselves surrounded by darkness and uncertainty.

We identify with the psalmist when he writes, "Why am I discouraged? Why is my heart so sad?" (Psalm 42:5).

There are times when we just feel distant from God. In the middle of our distress, we pray, looking for an answer, but we hear nothing but the echoes of our own voices. Like the psalmist, we cry out, "O God my rock…why have you forgotten me?" (Psalm 42:9).

Other times we lose the joy of our salvation because of our own spiritual apathy. The mystics call this *acedia,* an old word that suggests spiritual indifference, both to our own lives and the lives of others. I've been in this state, and so have you. Writing in a time before social media, Richard John Neuhaus explains, "Acedia is evenings without number obliterated by television, evenings neither of entertainment nor of education but of narcoticized defense against time and duty."[1]

Sometimes the darkness we experience is no fault of our own. We are the victims of circumstance, or perhaps we have been falsely accused. One December in my family's Christian bookstore, a man came in and created a disturbance. After trying to reason with him, we had no choice but to remove the interloper. The man ended up suing our business and me personally, claiming we had violated his rights.

The case dragged on for two years, and much to our surprise and dismay, it went to a civil trial with a judge and jury. Our business and its ministry were at stake. This was a dark time for my wife and me. We were in the deep, feeling like we were sinking and going down, yet not so low that we did not feel God's mercy and love. In fact, as the process dragged on, we entered a place of calm and assurance. I had not felt anything like it before, and nothing since has equaled that inner peace and assurance of being held in the arms of God as the waves and breakers swept over us.

By God's grace the jury ruled in our favor and there was no judgment against us. To this day I can clearly remember the overwhelming feeling of gratitude for God's special care as the verdict was read. At that moment my wife and I sensed a deep bond to our loving Father.

There's another reason why we come to this place of deep calling to deep: We long for a deeper moving of the Holy Spirit in our lives. We have read about his power in the pages of Scripture and history, and we have heard about his power in the lives of others in our world today. And we wonder, *How do I appropriate and unleash this power in my own life?*

BACK TO THE UPPER ROOM

I want to take you back to the night Jesus was betrayed, when he shared a last meal with his disciples, so you can see how he answered this question. This night is as deep and dark as it gets, on a personal as well as cosmic level. After washing the feet of his disciples, Jesus makes two predictions: Someone will betray him, and his most passionate and impetuous disciple will deny him (John 13:21-38).

And yet, in the midst of this place of despair and confusion, there is hope beyond all measure for those who have given everything to follow Jesus. In a series of seven remarkable statements recorded in John 14, Jesus reveals the powerful truth of his identity and what he is about to do.

- He is going to prepare a place in heaven for them (verses 1-4).

- He is the way, the truth, and the life, and the only way to the Father (verse 6).

- To know him is to know God (verse 7).

- Anyone who has seen him has seen the Father (verse 9).

- Whoever believes in him will do greater works than he did (verse 12).

- His followers can ask anything in his name, and he will do it (verse 14).

- He will send another advocate—the Spirit of truth (verses 16-17).

YOUR FIRST ADVOCATE

There is a wonderful chapter in Tim Keller's book *Encounters with Jesus* called "The Two Advocates." As Keller explains, the word *advocate* means "to be sympathetic, to be in a relationship, to stand in someone's shoes."[2] Jesus is our first Advocate, filling this role in his position in heaven at the right hand of the Father, where he is interceding for us (Romans 8:34; Hebrews 7:25).

I used to think this meant Jesus has my back by pleading my case to God, even when I make mistakes. But I have learned this is not exactly right. As my Advocate, Jesus does more than whisper in God's ear, "Hey, Stan is a pretty good guy." That view trivializes what Jesus did for me on the cross. "When you put your faith in Jesus," Keller writes, "when you say from the heart, 'Father, accept me because of what

Jesus did,' then Jesus' work on the cross is transferred to your account."[3] Here is how Paul expresses this profound truth:

> God made Christ, who never sinned, to be the offering for our sin, so that we could be made right with God through Christ (2 Corinthians 5:21).

As my first Advocate, here's what Jesus says to the Father about me: "See what I've done. And now, accept Stan in me."[4]

ANOTHER ADVOCATE

When Jesus told his disciples he would send "another Advocate," he left no doubt concerning this Advocate's identity—the Spirit of truth (John 14:17). We talked about this special role of the Holy Spirit in chapter 4, and it's true that he teaches and guides us into all truth as we read and study God's Word. But he does much more, as Jesus explains:

> When he comes, he will convict the world of its sin, and of God's righteousness, and of the coming judgment. The world's sin is that it refuses to believe in me (John 16:8-9).

As our second Advocate, the Holy Spirit convicts us. Yes, he will teach us deep truth, but "he will not merely hold [our] hand or give [us] energy," as Keller says. He will also help us see the gravity of our sin—not to make us feel bad, but to tell us that apart from Christ, we can do nothing.

Your first Advocate makes you right before God. As Keller says, he speaks to *God* for you. Your second Advocate, on the other hand, speaks to *you* for you. He helps you see your sin that God has forgiven in Christ, prompting you to live "with the humility and dependence on God that results from that fact."[5]

The Holy Spirit also intercedes for us, especially when we don't know what to pray for. His prayers for us are deep and passionate, "with groanings that cannot be expressed in words" (Romans 8:26). And the Holy Spirit always prays "in harmony with God's own will" (verse 27), which gives us this beautiful picture of all three members of the Trinity engaged on our behalf when we pray. The pattern of prayer I have been taught is to pray to the Father in the name of Jesus and in the power of the Holy Spirit. But as I have become more acquainted with the Holy Spirit, I have begun to ask him to help me, since I don't always know what to pray for.

The disciples in the upper room may not have grasped these deep truths that night, but they came to recognize the power and purpose of what Jesus told them when they witnessed his death, resurrection, and ascension, and then received the baptism of the Holy Spirit on the day of Pentecost. These timid, trembling followers who had failed Jesus in life would turn the world upside down (Acts 17:6 ESV). When the power of the Holy Spirit came upon them, they became his witnesses in Jerusalem, Judea, Samaria, "and to the ends of the earth" (Acts 1:8).

CAN YOU HAVE
WHAT THEY HAD?

When we read about the disciples in the New Testament, says Lloyd-Jones, we see "this power, this joy, this abandon, this thrill." And then we ask, "Are we like that?"[6] It would be easy to conclude that the first century was a unique time in history, when the good-news message of Jesus Christ was carried into the world for the first time by a small group of Christ followers. It was a time when these disciples—later called "apostles" because they were "sent out"—had the supernatural power of the Holy Spirit at their disposal.

But the great commission Jesus gave after his resurrection, and the pronouncement of power with the Holy Spirit he gave before his ascension, are both still in effect. The commission of Jesus and the Holy Spirit's power are as real and relevant today as they have ever been. As we look back over the last 2,000 years, we can see periods of great revival and reformation, spurred on by the Holy Spirit, as well as times of spiritual lethargy. So, where are we now?

I would contend that we are about to enter a time of spiritual renewal unlike anything the world has seen. Already in our lifetimes we have witnessed the rapid growth of the church in China and the global South, and yet I believe the best is yet to come. Here are three reasons why:

1. **Technology.** We are experiencing the greatest technological revolution in the last 500 years. In the mid-1400s, Gutenberg's printing press changed the world because it brought content and books, including the Bible, to the masses. Today, we are witnessing a new kind of revolution fueled by digital technology, and once again it is bringing content and books, including the Bible, to the masses. Just as God was behind the printing press, he is behind the technological marvels we have

today. The big difference, of course, is that in the fifteenth century there were about 500 million people on the planet. Today, there are more than 7 billion people.

2. **Bible translation.** There are approximately 7,000 "heart" languages in the world. So far, at least some of the Bible has been translated into nearly half of them. Thanks to digital technology and new coordinated efforts on the part of Bible societies and translation ministries around the world, Bible translation efforts have accelerated. It is estimated that virtually every person on the planet will have a Bible in their own language by 2033.

3. **Globalization.** Tomas Larsson, a Swedish journalist, defines this term as "the process of world shrinkage, of distances getting shorter, things moving closer. It pertains to the increasing ease with which somebody on one side of the world can interact, to mutual benefit, with somebody on the other side of the world."[7]

As you consider these three realities in our world today and overlay them with the great commission and the "you will receive power" pronouncement of Jesus (Acts 1:8), you can't help but believe we live in a historic moment unlike any other—both for the world and also for the gospel. If ever the eyes of God were searching the whole earth "in order to strengthen those whose hearts are fully committed to him" (2 Chronicles 16:9), it is now. He is searching for those who are willing to step into this moment, when people from every tribe and nation are looking for hope beyond themselves, to bring them the saving message of Jesus Christ.

Do you have something gnawing at your spirit? Do you feel a restlessness that won't go away? Perhaps you can relate to these words written by Lloyd-Jones several decades ago:

> I should not be like this, I must not remain like this. I see that there is this other possibility and I want that, I want to be like that. I see the need of this and I see the urgency of this need.[8]

YOU WILL RECEIVE POWER

There are those who are satisfied with the way things are, but there are many who are restless. Are you among them? You know you cannot do this alone. You need help. You need the power of the Holy Spirit.

Are you in a position to receive this power promised by Jesus? As introduced in the last chapter, Lloyd-Jones suggests four steps we must take to appropriate the Holy Spirit's power.

Need

Recognizing the need and its urgency seem pretty obvious, but our perspective must go beyond our own preferences. We need to consider what God is already doing in the world through the church.

I have a friend who is the pastor of a large church in Southern California. He could have been content to minister to his growing congregation, but God stirred his heart to also provide resources for pastors in Ethiopia, where the church is growing at an astounding rate.

He had never written a book before, but he decided to write one that would teach and train pastors. The Holy Spirit empowered my friend not just to write and publish the book, but also to arrange for it to be translated into Oromo, the most common first language in Ethiopia. The book was such a success that the government helped to distribute it throughout the country. And he did all this while still serving as the pastor of his local church, all because the power of the Holy Spirit was upon him.

I'm guessing that you already have the sense of a need stirring in your heart. It may seem like an impossible dream, but you can't get it out of your heart and mind. Bring it before the Lord in prayer. Research and study the need. Talk to spiritually mature people about it. Ask the Holy Spirit to give you insights, courage, and open doors. You will be amazed at what he will do. But before you can go on, there are other things to consider.

Motive

Lloyd-Jones says there will always be those who become interested in the Holy Spirit because they want a "fresh experience," but most of the time they are only concerned about power. In fact, they covet power. "We do need power," says Lloyd-Jones, "but…if you isolate it and are merely concerned that you should have power, you put yourself into a very dangerous position."[9] The Holy Spirit gives experiences and power, but that's not what we should be seeking.

So what should we seek? The one whom the Holy Spirit always points to: Jesus Christ. The apostle Paul had this as his highest ambition, and it should be ours as well:

> Whatever were gains to me I now consider loss
> for the sake of Christ. What is more, I consider
> everything a loss because of the surpassing worth
> of knowing Christ Jesus my Lord, for whose sake
> I have lost all things (Philippians 3:7-8 NIV).

This motive to know Jesus is not something we can conjure up on our own without one more element, and that's love. I have found it impossible to be motivated to do anything—whether it's knowing Christ Jesus or getting better at my job—unless love is at the core. I know, it sounds idealistic. You can probably think of goals you have set for yourself that involved discipline, mental toughness, and inner resolve. Yes, those factors all contribute to your motive, but the greatest motivator of all is love.

"For the love of the game" is a phrase that motivates athletes to excel. True love is what motivated Westley to sacrifice everything in order to rescue Buttercup in *The Princess Bride*. "For God so loved the world" is the reason he gave us his only Son (John 3:16 NIV). That's why the apostle Paul reached this conclusion: "The greatest of these is love" (1 Corinthians 13:13).

But we are flawed people, and our love, as wonderful and universal as it is, cannot be manufactured or contrived. We can't love the Lord our God with all our heart, soul, mind, and strength on our own. We need help. Once again the Holy Spirit comes to our rescue by helping us to love. Here's how Paul expresses this supernatural bestowal of love:

> We know how dearly God loves us, because he has
> given us the Holy Spirit to fill our hearts with his
> love (Romans 5:5).

As you consider your motive to fill a need God has made known to you, examine your heart to confirm that you are doing it out of love. If not, then whatever need you are thinking about is not a need God wants you to fulfill. The emphasis in Scripture is always on love, starting with loving God with all your heart, soul, mind, and strength, and then loving others. This is the "greatest commandment" that Jesus gave to his followers (Matthew 22:37-40).

Lloyd-Jones calls this principle of love the "pneumatic element" that has characterized the church in all periods of revival and reawakening over the last twenty centuries.

> That is what we must seek—not experiences, not power, not gifts. If he chooses to give them to us, thank God for them and exercise them to his glory, but the only safe way of receiving gifts is that you love him and that you know him.[10]

Obedience

After the Holy Spirit comes in power to the believers on the day of Pentecost, amazing things start to happen. With an eye for detail and a sense of the dramatic, Luke the physician observes and writes about one wondrous event after another in the book of Acts.

The believers speak in other languages; Peter preaches a message of repentance to a crowd; and 3,000 people are baptized and added to the church. The apostles perform many signs and wonders, and the believers begin sharing everything they have with one another. As they watch God work in their midst through the power of the Holy Spirit, "a deep sense of awe" overcomes them (Acts 2:43).

Peter heals a lame beggar and is again prompted to preach to a crowd watching in amazement. All of this miraculous activity catches the attention of the religious leaders, who are disturbed by Peter and his fellow apostle John, who are preaching about the resurrected Christ. They arrest the apostles and demand that they no longer speak to anyone in Jesus' name, but this only emboldens Peter and John. Their declaration reverberates throughout history: "Do you think God wants us to obey you rather than him? We cannot stop telling about everything we have seen and heard" (Acts 4:19-20).

This theme of obedience recurs throughout the book of Acts. Obeying God is not about disobeying laws meant to help and protect people. But when believers are told to stop talking about Jesus, there is only one way to respond: "We must obey God rather than any human authority" (Acts 5:29).

The apostles were motivated by love—love for God, love for one another, and love for those who needed the salvation only Jesus can provide (Acts 4:11-12). By their lives they demonstrated that love always expresses itself in terms of obedience.

Once the Holy Spirit regenerates and indwells us, he begins his work in us. He continues to convict us concerning sin, guides us into the truth of Scripture, reveals the supernatural gifts he has given us, and empowers us to use those gifts. Yet, despite these promptings, the result is not automatic. We have a choice to obey or not obey the Holy Spirit. If we obey, he will continue to convict, guide, enlighten, and empower us. If we deliberately ignore his promptings, he will stop working in us because he is grieved (Ephesians 4:30). We must do everything we can to neither grieve nor quench the Spirit.

Instead, we must choose to obey no matter what happens,

no matter what the cost, because we understand the reality of who we are and whose we are.

> You do not belong to yourself, for God bought
> you with a high price (1 Corinthians 6:19-20).

This is what Peter and John and the early church believed. This is how they lived, and it's how we should live, with obedience that is all about abandonment of ourselves to God and to his gracious purposes. The need and our motive are nothing without obedience to the God who loves us, the Son who saved us, and the Holy Spirit who empowers us. As Lloyd-Jones observes, "You show the depth of your desire by the extent of your obedience."[11]

Prayer

You would think that prayer would be the first step in any spiritual endeavor, and indeed it should be. It's always a good idea to pray, whether at the beginning, middle, or end of something. However, the prayer we're going to talk about now is at a different level. This is serious prayer.

Over the years I have observed that people sometimes treat prayer like it's a right rather than a privilege. I've been guilty of this. We pray as if we're in charge and God is somehow obligated to answer. When you think about this in the context of everything we have been discussing in this book, it's not a bold approach, but a presumptuous one.

We never want to presume on God. We have no claims on him. We can't demand anything of him. Anything he gives us is a gift, not an obligation. We can never say to God, "I have paid the price, now give me what I want." As Lloyd-Jones says, you just don't deal with God in this way. Instead, as we approach God in prayer, we should say, as Lloyd-Jones suggests, "I am an unprofitable servant; I am dependent solely upon the grace, the free grace of God and his mercy and his love and his compassion."[12]

So how do we pray for this blessing, this baptism, this power of the Holy Spirit? Lloyd-Jones suggests a phrase that probably sounds a bit antiquated: "You plead the promises." You rarely hear this kind of praying now, writes Jones.

> Why? Because people do not really pray any longer, they send little telegrams to God. They think that that is the height of spirituality. They know nothing about "wrestling" with God and "pleading the promises."[13]

In my reading of the lives and books of Moody, Murray, Simpson, Torrey, and Tozer, I found autobiographical examples of their "pleading the promises," waiting on God to give them the blessing and power to accomplish some purpose he has in mind for them. Even more, I see the example of Jesus, who pleaded the promises of God in a prayer that teaches us more about submitting to God's will and purposes than any other in Scripture:

> Father, if you are willing, please take this cup of suffering away from me. Yet I want your will to be done, not mine (Luke 22:42).

In light of this example, the question we need to ask ourselves is this: *Am I willing to surrender all in order for God to do his work through me?*

NOW WHAT?

Having outlined four steps to discerning and receiving the blessing and baptism of the Holy Spirit (with acknowledgment to Martyn Lloyd-Jones), I now want to give you four caveats.

First, these four steps are not a formula. It would be easy to develop a checklist and move from one step to the next, but there's more to this than simply following a process. Yes, there is an order to these steps, but that is for our benefit, not God's. There will be times when you do them all at once, or one and not the other. And you will never follow these steps perfectly.

Second, there are no shortcuts. We are all impatient, especially in this era of instant answers and immediate gratification. It takes time for God to make each of us into someone he can use. Joseph was sold into slavery and spent years in prison before God elevated him to a place of influence. Moses was in the wilderness for 40 years before God called him to free his people. Paul did not rush his ministry after his conversion (see Galatians 1:16–2:2). What makes us think we are ready now?

Third, we think we can start from where we are, when generally we cannot. Based on our own experience and the experiences of others we have known or read of, including every biblical character God used for his purposes, we can be sure of this. We have to be taken down; we have to be humbled; we may even have to be humiliated. Only then will God deal with us in the most incredible ways.[14]

Finally, as we take this journey, we should be ready for spiritual warfare. "The moment you enter that realm," Lloyd-Jones writes, "the devil is obviously going to be disturbed… The moment you have these longings and desires for something bigger and deeper, then the devil will attack you."[15]

I'm not saying we should look for demons behind every corner, but we should take spiritual warfare seriously. The Bible is clear that Satan roams the earth like a roaring lion, seeking someone to devour (1 Peter 5:8). And his demons disguise themselves as "servants of righteousness" (2 Corinthians 11:15). They live to distract us and lead us to spiritual error. We need to train ourselves through study, prayer, and practice "to recognize the difference between right and wrong" (Hebrews 5:14).

We also need to recognize the difference between a false spirit and the Holy Spirit. It's pretty simple, as long as we never forget the one big thing: The Holy Spirit always points to Jesus Christ (1 John 4:2).

Above all, we need not fear. Instead, we can plead this promise from Scripture:

> You belong to God, my dear children. You have already won a victory over those people, because the Spirit who lives in you is greater than the spirit who lives in the world (1 John 4:4).

Epilogue

When I was a freshman at Bible college, I took a New Testament Survey class. In the first 15 minutes of the first class, the professor read a verse that puzzled me:

> All of us who have had that veil removed can see
> and reflect the glory of the Lord. And the Lord—
> who is the Spirit—makes us more and more like
> him as we are changed into his glorious image
> (2 Corinthians 3:18).

But now, as I have committed to give more of myself to the Holy Spirit, the meaning and application of Paul's words have come into focus. The picture of the "veil" comes from Moses, whose face shone with the reflected glory of God after he had spoken to him. Moses wore the veil, not to protect the people from the Lord's radiance, but to prevent them from seeing that the glory was fading.

The glory that Moses reflected was a diminishing radiance

because it was based on "the old way, which brings condemnation" (2 Corinthians 3:9). By contrast, we can expect a "far greater glory under the new way, now that the Holy Spirit is giving life" (2 Corinithains 3:8). The glory on Moses' face was transitory. The glory a believer reflects is eternal because of God's abiding presence through the Holy Spirit.

> Whenever someone turns to the Lord, the veil is taken away. For the Lord is the Spirit, and wherever the Spirit of the Lord is, there is freedom (2 Corinthians 3:16-17).

This is what the Holy Spirit does in our lives. As he produces fruit, we are progressively being transformed into the likeness of Jesus as we give him glory. In other words, the "one big thing" the Holy Spirit does becomes our "one big thing," thanks to the fire and wind of the Holy Spirit.

Writing this book has been a journey of discovery for me. I hope and pray that reading this book has set you on a journey of your own, one that will take you into the depths of God, where you go beyond your own ability to that place where you are totally dependent on the Father, Son, and Holy Spirit.

This doesn't mean you live in a state of euphoric disconnection from everything around you. Quite the opposite. By walking in the Spirit, you will be keenly aware of the circumstances and people around you. Rather than following your own selfish desires, your Spirit-filled life will naturally cause you to love others and have a deep desire to help them.

The fire and wind of the Holy Spirit are available to you every day as you surrender to him. Give it a try and watch what happens. I have no doubt God will use you in remarkable ways as his power and presence are unleashed in your life.

The world is desperately in need of hope—the hope that comes only from the love of God, accomplished by the person and work of Jesus Christ, and applied in our lives by the Holy Spirit. It's always been this way, but we are more aware than any past generation of the cries for hope coming from people in our own communities and from every corner of the world. We read their stories and see their images on our phones.

We can't get away from the desperation of many people today, nor can we ignore it. The physical and emotional needs of those without hope are overwhelming on their own, but the spiritual needs of people around us are even more acute.

When Jesus traveled through the towns and villages, people in great numbers would gather to hear his teaching and seek his healing. On one particular occasion, when Jesus saw the crowds, "he had compassion on them because they were confused and helpless, like sheep without a shepherd" (Matthew 9:36).

Jesus then turned to his disciples and said, "The harvest is great, but the workers are few. So pray to the Lord who is in charge of the harvest; ask him to send more workers into his fields" (Matthew 9:37-38).

May we have hearts like Jesus that break for those who are harassed and without hope. The number of hopeless people in the world is beyond comprehension. Even those around us who need Jesus are beyond our natural ability to help. We need supernatural power.

This is where the Helper steps in. The Holy Spirit is not a presence in our lives for our benefit alone. He desires to work in us and through us, leveraging our spiritual gifts as we share the good news with others and serve them in a supernatural way as his agents of hope and healing.

The Holy Spirit is more than a warm feeling in our hearts. He is the Spirit of Jesus calling us to bring hope to the world.

The Authors in the Box

Andrew Murray (1828–1917) was a South African writer, teacher, and pastor. His father was a Dutch Reformed Church missionary to South Africa. Murray was a leader in the South African Revival of 1860 and one of the founders of the South African General Mission, which began in 1889 and continues to this day as part of SIM. Murray wrote dozens of books, including the classic *The Indwelling Spirit*. Because of his theology of healing and his belief in the continuation of apostolic gifts, Murray is considered a forerunner of the Pentecostal movement.

Dwight Lyman Moody (1837–1899) was an American evangelist, educator, and publisher with ties to the Holiness movement. His conversion at the age of 18 launched his lifetime passion for evangelism. He was a popular evangelist in the United States and England, where Charles Spurgeon befriended and promoted him. Despite a meager upbringing and the lack of a formal education, Moody founded Illinois Street Church and the Chicago Evangelization Society, renamed Moody Church and Moody Bible Institute, respectively, after his death. In 1894 he founded Moody Publishers to produce affordable Christian books.

Albert Benjamin Simpson (1843–1919) was a Canadian preacher, theologian, author, hymn writer, and the founder of the Christian and Missionary Alliance denomination, including a related college and seminary. His Christ-centered theology became known as the Fourfold Gospel: Jesus as Savior, Sanctifier, Healer, and Coming King. At the beginning of the twentieth century, Simpson became involved in the Pentecostal movement.

Reuben Archer Torrey (1856–1928) was an American pastor and educator and the author of more than 40 books. A graduate of Yale University and Yale Divinity School, he started churches and then became the superintendent of what is now the Moody Bible Institute and pastor of what is now Moody Church. In 1912 Torrey accepted the position of dean of the Bible Institute of Los Angeles, now Biola University. He was also a world-renowned evangelist, preaching in China, Japan, and India, along with nearly every part of the English-speaking world.

Aiden Wilson Tozer (1897–1963) was an American pastor, author, and magazine editor. Although he was born into poverty and self-educated, Tozer was the pastor of several churches, including Southside Alliance in Chicago, where he served for 30 years. He also served as the editor of the *Alliance Weekly*, the official publication of the Christian and Missionary Alliance. Tozer was the author of more than 60 books, many compiled after his death from his sermons and articles. Two of his books, *The Pursuit of God* and *The Knowledge of the Holy*, are considered Christian classics.

Comments on Pronouns and Gender

PRONOUNS

In this book you will find a slight inconsistency in the personal pronouns used for God, Jesus, and the Holy Spirit—as in *he*, *him*, and *his*. You will notice that I do not capitalize these pronouns. The reason for this is so the text is consistent with the majority of Bible translations, which do not capitalize them either, since the original Hebrew and Greek manuscripts do not capitalize these words.

By comparison, you will notice that the five "authors in the box" I quote throughout the book capitalize pronouns for God, primarily because that was the practice when most of their books were written.

GENDER

The Bible uses the masculine gender to describe God the Father, Jesus the Son, and the Holy Spirit. Technically, only Jesus is male. Both God and the Holy Spirit are, well, *Spirit*. God is neither male nor female because he is not human. Neither is the Holy Spirit. But in Scripture we are instructed to call God our Father (something Jesus does as well), and the Holy Spirit is always referred to in the masculine. But this does not mean the Holy Spirit is a man any more than God is a man. In fact, neither God nor the Holy Spirit has a body.

What all three members of the Trinity do have are human qualities. Or, more correctly, we humans have qualities that the triune God possesses. That's because God created us in *his* image. Of course, we don't look like God physically (again, he's not a human), but we share the emotional qualities that God the Father, Jesus the Son, and the Holy Spirit possess.

And it's not just God the Father who made us this way. All three members of the Trinity were active in the creation of humanity: "Let us make human beings in our image, to be like us," the Bible tells us (Genesis 1:26).

Notes

INTRODUCTION

1. A.W. Tozer, *Alive In the Spirit* (Minneapolis, MN: Bethany House, 2016), 63.

2. Andrew Murray, *Experiencing the Holy Spirit* (New Kensington, PA: Whitaker House, 1985), 13.

3. D.L. Moody, *Secret Power* (New Kensington, PA: Whitaker House, 1997), 91.

4. A.B. Simpson, *Days of Heaven Upon Earth* (New York, NY: Christian Alliance Publishing Co.), August 5.

5. R.A. Torrey, *The Person and Work of the Holy Spirit* (Grand Rapids, MI: Zondervan, 1974), 10.

6. A.W. Tozer, *The Pursuit of God* (Ventura, CA: Regal Books, 2013), 64.

7. Calvin Miller, *Into the Depths of God* (Bloomington, MN: Bethany House, 2000), 119.

CHAPTER 1

1. A.W. Tozer, *Alive in the Spirit*, ed. James. L Snyder (Bloomington, MN: Bethany House, 2016), 30.

2. Simpson, *Holy Spirit: or Power from on High* (New York, NY: The Christian Alliance Publishing Co., 1895), vol. 1, chapter 2, "The Breath of God."

3. Torrey, *Person and Work*, 10.

4. Tozer, *Alive in the Spirit*, 30.

5. Torrey, *Person and Work*, 112.

6. Tim Chester, *Enjoying God* (Charlotte, NC: The Good Book Company, 2018), 173.

7. Catherine Marshall, *The Helper* (Grand Rapids, MI: Chosen, 2001), 21.

8. Murray, *Experiencing the Holy Spirit*, 38.

9. Torrey, *Person and Work*, 10.

10. From a modern translation of the Nicene Creed.

11. Torrey, *Person and Work*, 47-48.

12. Tozer, *Alive in the Spirit*, 65.

CHAPTER 2

1. Torrey, *Person and Work*, 69.

2. Tozer, *Alive in the Spirit*, 68.

3. Ibid.

4. Ibid., 69.

5. Ibid., 75,77.

6. Dictionary.com, s.v. "regeneration," https://www.dictionary.com/browse/regeneration.

7. Torrey, *Person and Work*, 94.

8. Kelly M. Kapic, *The God Who Gives*, with Justin L. Borger (Grand Rapids, MI: Zondervan, 2018), 136.

CHAPTER 3

1. Tozer, *Alive in the Spirit*, 170.

2. Torrey, *Person and Work*, 94.

3. Tozer, *Alive in the Spirit*, 165.

4. D.L. Moody, *Secret Power* (Shawnee, KS: Gideon House, 2015), 35.

5. Simpson, *Holy Spirit: or Power from on High* (New York, NY: The Christian Alliance Publishing Co., 1896), vol.2, chapter 2, "The Holy Spirit in Galatians," section VI.

6. John R.W. Stott, *The Message of Galatians* (Downers Grove, IL: IVP Academic, 1968), 148.

7. Simpson, Holy Spirit, vol. 2, chapter 14, "The Holy Spirit in Galatians," section VII.

8. Tozer, *Alive in the Spirit,* 167.

9. N.T. Wright, *Simply Christian* (San Francisco, CA: HarperOne, 2010), 124.

CHAPTER 4

1. Simpson, *Holy Spirit*, vol. 2, chapter 19, "The Holy Spirit in the Epistles of Paul to Timothy," section II.

2. R.A. Torrey, *How to Obtain Fullness of Power* (New Kensington, PA: Whitaker House, 2002), 62.

3. Jordan Standridge, "Why You Desperately Need the Holy Spirit," *The Cripplegate,* February 6, 2018, http://thecripplegate.com/why-you-desperately-need-the-holy-spirit.

4. Torrey, *Person and Work*, 123.

5. Simpson, *Holy Spirit,* vol.2, chapter 6, "The Comforter," section VI.

6. Torrey, *Person and Work*, 121.

7. Moody, *Secret Power*, 29.

8. Wright, *Simply Christian,* 181.

9. John Piper, *Reading the Bible Supernaturally* (Wheaton, IL: Crossway, 2017), 180.

10. Ibid., 209.

11. Paul E. Miller, *A Praying Life* (Colorado Springs, CO: NavPress, 2017), 252.

12. Scot McKnight, *Open to the Spirit* (Colorado Springs, CO: WaterBrook, 2018), 29.

13. Miller, *A Praying Life*, 252.

14. McKnight, *Open to the Spirit*, 33.

15. Bruce Bickel and Stan Jantz, *Bruce and Stan's Pocket Guide to Studying Your Bible* (Eugene, OR: Harvest House, 2001), 33-35.

CHAPTER 5

1. C.S. Lewis, *The Weight of Glory* (San Francisco, CA: HarperOne, 2001), 45.

2. Wayne Grudem, *Systematic Theology* (Grand Rapids, MI: Zondervan, 1994), 1016.

3. Tozer, *Alive in the Spirit*, 92.

4. Ibid., 93.

5. Simpson, *Holy Spirit*, vol.2, chapter 12, "The Holy Spirit in the Body of Christ," section I.

6. Tozer, *Alive in the Spirit*, 93.

7. Ibid., 94-95.

8. Ibid., 96.

9. Ibid., 97.

10. Bruce Bickel and Stan Jantz, *Bruce and Stan's Pocket Guide to Knowing the Holy Spirit* (Eugene, OR: Harvest House, 2002), 94-102.

11. A.J. Gordon, *The Ministry of Healing* (London: Hodder and Stoughton, 1882), 28-29,33.

12. A.B. Simpson, *The Gospel of Healing* (Harrisburg, PA: Christian Publications, 1915), 162-63.

CHAPTER 6

1. Matthew Henry, *Matthew Henry's Commentary on the Whole Bible* (1706), Ezekiel 47, http://www.biblestudytools.com/commentaries/matthew-henry-complete/ezekiel/47.html.

2. Alan Carr, "At the Mercy of the River," *The Sermon Notebook*, accessed May 8, 2019, http://www.sermonnotebook.org/old%20testament/Ezekiel%2047_1-12.htm.

3. Henry, *Matthew Henry's Commentary*.

4. Torrey, *Person and Work*, 150.

5. Ibid., 154-55.

6. Martyn Lloyd-Jones, *Joy Unspeakable*, ed. Christopher Catherwood (Wheaton, IL: Harold Shaw, 1985), 77.

7. Ibid., 77,81.

8. D.L. Moody, as quoted in William Revell Moody, *The Life of Dwight L. Moody* (Cambridge, MA: Andover-Harvard Theological Library, 1910), 149.

9. Murray, *Experiencing the Holy Spirit*, 41.

10. Lloyd-Jones, *Joy Unspeakable*, 84-85.

11. Torrey, *Person and Work*, 165,180.

12. Lloyd-Jones, *Joy Unspeakable*, 115-18.

13. A.J. Gordon, *The Holy Spirit in Missions* (New York, NY: Fleming H. Revell, 1893), 209-10.

14. Hudson Taylor to Berger, in Dr. and Mrs. Howard Taylor, *Hudson Taylor's Spiritual Secret* (Chicago, IL: Moody, 2009), 179.

15. Lloyd-Jones, *Joy Unspeakable*, 207.

16. Ibid., 208.

17. Ibid., 210.

CHAPTER 7

1. Richard John Neuhaus, *Freedom for Ministry* (Grand Rapids, MI: William B. Eerdmans, 1992), 227.

2. Timothy Keller, *Encounters with Jesus* (New York, NY: Penguin, 2015), 131.

3. Ibid., 140.

4. Ibid., 141.

5. Ibid., 141-42.

6. Lloyd-Jones, *Joy Unspeakable*, 199.

7. Tomas Larsson, *The Race to the Top* (Washington, DC: Cato Institute, 2001), 9.

8. Lloyd-Jones, *Joy Unspeakable*, 199.

9. Ibid., 200-01.

10. Ibid., 203.

11. Ibid., 207.

12. Ibid.

13. Ibid., 208-09.

14. Ibid., 221.

15. Ibid., 219.

ABOUT THE AUTHOR

Stan Jantz is the president of the Evangelical Christian Publishers Association and cofounder of ConversantLife.com. He is the coauthor of more than 50 books, including *Now That You're a Christian, Bible Answers 101,* and other books in the Christianity 101® series. He makes his home in Huntington Beach, California.

Books by Bruce Bickel
and Stan Jantz

Knowing the Bible 101
With extensive biblical knowledge and a contemporary perspective, Bruce Bickel and Stan Jantz provide a manageable approach to understanding God's written message—its origin, themes, truth, and personal relevance.

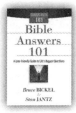

Bible Answers 101
Bruce and Stan gather and answer more than 200 tough questions they've been asked about the Christian faith. Why is grace important if we believe we're saved? What happens when we die? Is Christ the only way to salvation? Readers will appreciate the sincere questions and the clear answers.

Now That You're a Christian
New believers will immediately connect with Bruce and Stan's honest, encouraging responses to questions new Christians often ask. Readers will discover what God has done for humanity, how people can know Him better, and how individuals can reflect the love of Christ to the world.

Growing as a Christian 101
In this fresh new look at the essentials of the Christian walk, Bruce and Stan offer readers the encouragement they need to continue making steady progress in their spiritual lives.

To learn more about Harvest House books and
to read sample chapters, visit our website:

www.harvesthousepublishers.com

HARVEST HOUSE PUBLISHERS
EUGENE, OREGON